The First Farmers

The Emergence of Man

The First Farmers

by Jonathan Norton Leonard
and the Editors
of Time-Life Books

TIME
LIFE
BOOKS

Time-Life International
(Nederland) B.V.

The Author: JONATHAN NORTON LEONARD is a freelance writer and a former staff writer for TIME-LIFE BOOKS. For 20 years he was Science Editor of TIME. He is the author of *Ancient America* and *Early Japan* in TIME-LIFE BOOKS' Great Ages of Man series and *The World of Gainsborough* in the TIME-LIFE Library of Art. Mr. Leonard was also one of the co-authors of *Life Before Man*, an earlier volume in The Emergence of Man series.

The Consultant: ROBERT H. DYSON JR., Professor of Anthropology and Curator of the Near Eastern Section of the University Museum at the University of Pennsylvania, has been expedition director for the University's excavation at Tepe Hasanlu, in Iran, during the digging seasons of alternate years since 1965. He has also directed the University's project in Guatemala, participating in the restoration of temples and palaces of the great Mayan city of Tikal.

The Cover: Ancient farmers of the Middle East harvest a ripe stand of newly domesticated wheat. Using flint-edged sickles made of bone, they toss their harvest into woven baskets. Because the wheat is so recently developed from the wild variety, which scatters its seeds easily, the men and women take care to hold the topmost, grain-bearing part of the plant as they cut it. The figures were painted by Burt Silverman on a photograph of Middle Eastern wheat that is almost exactly the same as that grown by the first farmers in 8000 B.C.

Contents

Introduction

Of all the cultural innovations created by man, certainly one of the most profound in its effects has been the invention of agriculture. This seemingly simple discovery of planting, cultivating and harvesting food provided the basis for larger populations and opened the way to all of the complex societies and higher civilizations that followed. Why and how it came about after more than a million years of hunting are questions that archaeologists and natural scientists are today trying to answer.

Although interest in the origin of food production is as old as the interest in prehistory itself, it is only in recent decades that intense research has been undertaken on the origins of farming. Research since 1948 has focused attention especially on the Middle East, where wheat and barley, sheep, goats, pigs and cattle had all been domesticated by about 6000 B.C.

Yet the very newness of this work imposes limitations on the reconstruction of what actually happened. Only a small number of sites have been excavated; furthermore, few have undergone the extensive clearance necessary for a complete understanding of the life and cultural activities of the farmers themselves.

Although research has so far concentrated on the initial steps in food production, the spread of agriculture is also an important study—with broad implications. The gradual expansion of the agricultural colonizers was not without cost. Game was driven off or killed, forests and grasslands were slashed and burned, ploughed up or overgrazed.

The arrival of the farmers meant the departure or gradual extinction of the bands of hunters and gatherers. With what dismay these simple hunters must have watched the transformation of their beloved hills and valleys, and with what distaste they must have viewed men willing to forgo their freedom of movement for the security of the barnyard!

The farmers, on the other hand, challenged by new needs and opportunities, must have welcomed the rise of amenities undreamed of previously, with an affluence potentially available for the community as a whole: surplus food not only to ensure the needs of the local people but to exchange with others for coveted objects and raw materials; innovations in technology and architecture; and systems of irrigation and improved transport.

Thus, farming activities not only caused a change in the countryside but they also fostered the growth of a biological and psychological environment that had formerly been experienced only in those rare areas where an accidental richness of wild-food resources had permitted large groups to settle permanently in one place.

With the rise of agriculture around the world, however, man had to deal increasingly with problems of sanitation, pollution and communicable disease, and psychologically he withdrew from the natural world into the more subtle and threatening world of unseen social pressures. Within the expanding complexities of this new social universe, with all its jealousies and passions, he had to redefine his relations to his fellow men and to the unseen forces around him. In the end, this need led to perhaps his greatest achievements: a conscious sense of moral order and the concept of law.

Robert H. Dyson Jr.
University Museum
University of Pennsylvania

Chapter One: The Middle East — Cradle of Agriculture

The few mud-walled, thatch-roofed huts stood in the bend of a shallow stream, a lonely cluster of life in an oak-dotted plain that sloped gently up to snowy mountains. As far as the eye could see, there was no other settlement. Downstream a flock of goats herded by a young boy was grazing on sun-shrivelled herbage. Closer to the village several women carrying baskets and holding wooden sickles set with sharp slivers of flint moved among irregular patches of tall yellow grass, each stalk of it tipped with double rows of tawny seeds. The grass—a primitive wheat—looked little different from similar grasses growing wild on the distant mountainsides. But it was different: it had been deliberately planted by the villagers, not sown haphazardly by the wind.

Suddenly a cry from the boy upset the village calm. The men picked up stone-tipped spears; the women working in the tall grass grabbed their partially filled baskets and began to run towards the village. What disturbed the villagers could be seen out on the plain: an approaching file of men, women and children —some 20 individuals in all. They were strangers, and their rugged appearance showed that they were hunters. One of the men had the carcass of a newly killed wild sheep slung over his shoulders. When the newcomers neared the stream bank opposite the village, they held up their hands to demonstrate their peaceful intent. They had not expected to find people living in mud huts where only a year before there

had been no dwellings at all—only a place for wanderers such as they to camp.

As nomads and villagers stood eyeing one another across the stream, one of the strangers pointed to the sheep carcass and then to the baskets of seeds. The villagers understood his meaning, and a woman brought a basket of wheat and set it down near the stream bank. The hunter carrying the sheep held up two fingers, and the woman placed a second basket beside the first. The strangers conferred in a huddle; then the hunter laid the carcass down. A man from the village waded across the stream with the two baskets of grain and touched the sheep lightly. The hunter touched the baskets in turn. The bargain was closed. The villager carried the sheep back to his people, and the wanderers shouldered the baskets of wheat and marched off among the oaks.

This encounter is of course imagined, but there is little doubt that it could have happened. There must have been many such episodes in the ancient Middle East when bands of nomadic hunter-gatherers exchanged wild game for villagers' grain and thus brushed against a marvel that would soon change the face of the earth. The villagers, crude and difficult though their life may have been, lived on another plane of existence. They were among the world's first farmers, people who had learned to cultivate a food-producing plant—not simply to gather naturally occurring plant food but to make it grow in a place where it did not grow ordinarily.

This seemingly simple advance first took place in about 8000 B.C. in the Middle East, somewhere in or near the Fertile Crescent, the hilly arc of inhabitable land that curves around the north of the empty Ara-

It was in hills like these in Israel that nomadic bands of hunter-gatherers began settling down 10,000 years ago. What attracted the wanderers to such areas was a bountiful supply of wild barley and wheat. Once they learned how to plant and raise these grains themselves, they ushered in a new way of life for mankind—farming, the basis of civilization.

bian Desert. Today the astonishing way in which this advance took place is becoming increasingly clear as archaeologists fine-comb the soil and sand of ancient agricultural sites. From the mud-walled ruins of farming villages that were far more advanced than anyone had even dreamed for so early a date, and from evidence as seemingly ephemeral as the husks of seeds and the bony cores of animal horns, the investigators have been able to piece together one of the greatest and most exciting episodes in human evolution, the birth of agriculture.

If it had not been for the first farmers, there would be no civilization today, and man would doubtless still be a hunter-gatherer, roaming the face of the earth in small bands. When those early agriculturists began domesticating wild wheat and barley and the sheep and goats on the hillsides around them, they were, in a sense, also domesticating themselves. Nothing as revolutionary had happened to man in a million years or more—certainly not since his Homo erectus ancestors had developed speech, mastered fire and learned to hunt together in effectively co-operating groups.

Within three or four thousand years after farming appeared in the Middle East, it was also invented independently in at least three other parts of the world, most notably North China, Mexico and Peru. Spreading from these centres to neighbouring regions, it worked a gradual but dramatic change in man's status on the planet.

Before the rise of farming and its related activity, the breeding of domestic animals, man was a rare and inconspicuous inhabitant of the earth. Like the other animals, he lived on the casual bounty of nature, adapting to the natural environment around him and changing it only in minor and transient ways in his efforts to increase his supplies of food.

Farming transformed man into an entirely different kind of organism: one with many other organisms —plants and animals—subjected to his will. His first hesitant steps in this direction produced amazing results. No longer did he merely adapt to the natural environment; now he began to alter it, and in major ways. Farming gave him the power to shift the balance of nature so that his own ecological system would provide more of what he needed. For example, by encouraging the growth of a relatively few food plants, like wheat and barley, the farmer at the same time discouraged many inedible wild plants that, unless weeded out of the fields, would absorb much of the moisture and many nutrients in the soil and might even choke out the food crops entirely. In much the same manner, he altered the balance of animal life in many areas, either by domesticating certain food-producing animals and directing their evolution or by discouraging the activities of other creatures that harmed his crops or killed his herds.

Finally, when the farmer had achieved an environment suited to his needs, he extended it to land where it could not naturally exist. In forest country, for instance, he cut down trees to open up space for the light-loving plants he cultivated; in arid regions he devised ways to bring the life-giving waters of rivers to acres that otherwise would yield nothing but scrubby brush. Eventually he even extended his man-made environment to steep mountainsides and, by carving them into terraces that would hold patches of soil, transformed them into productive farmland.

The result was the production of more food within a given area. And once man had a much larger food

Text continued on page 14

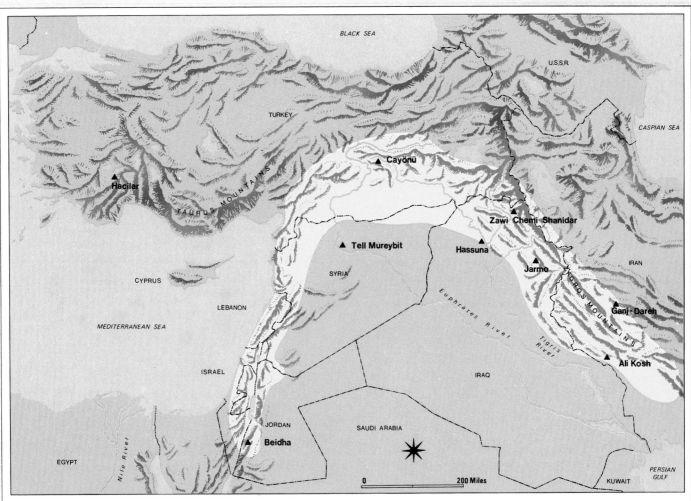

This topographical map of the Middle East shows the hilly flanks where agriculture began in 8000 B.C. and the overlapping territory where the barley and two types of wheat that the early farmers first domesticated still grow wild in massive stands (yellow area). The hilly flanks region is made up of the foothills of the Zagros and Taurus mountains and the uplands of northern Israel, and is so called because it flanks the fertile Crescent, the strip of productive land curving from Iran around Iraq and Syria to the Valley of the Nile. Sites of some of the villages associated with early farmers and referred to in the text are indicated by triangles.

Seen from a cave, the Jordan Valley, site of some of the earliest agricultural settlements in the world, unfolds below hills that even today suppo

stands of wild grain. Groups of prehistoric farmers were drawn from the sloping terrain into the valley by its patches of well-watered, fertile soil.

supply ready at hand, the groundwork was laid for civilization. The tempo of human life speeded up, as if an oxcart were hitched to a jet engine. Farming greatly accelerated developments that had already started to appear among certain hunter-gatherers living in favoured places: it encouraged permanent settlements in place of nomadic wanderings, inspired the invention of new tools and techniques, and stimulated the elaboration of arts and crafts. It triggered an explosive increase in population, encouraging not only larger families, but large and complex societies, which in turn fostered government, trade and communication among great numbers of people.

After the Neolithic Revolution, as anthropologists call the development of farming, man was no longer an inconspicuous rarity. Armed with his new skills and power, he became not simply the dominant animal on earth but the planet's dominant form of life.

Today farming feeds most of the world's inhabitants, but until 8000 B.C.—only yesterday in the million-year history of humanity—all people on earth were hunter-gatherers. Indeed, for something like 99 per cent of his time on earth, man led such an existence. In a few places where nature was especially bountiful the hunters settled down in villages, but the overwhelming majority lived in small bands that were forced to wander restlessly in search of food. When a band had killed or driven away most of the game animals in its vicinity and depleted more attractive vegetable foods, it went somewhere else, guided by knowledge of seasonal products and animal habits. For a long time scholars generally assumed that these ancient foragers led a precarious existence, forever hovering on the brink of starvation. A phrase of the 17th Century English philosopher Thomas Hobbes—that people in a state of nature lead "nasty, brutish and short" lives—was repeated in learned circles almost to the present day.

Actually, to judge from recent studies of existing hunter-gatherer societies, this way of life is not as bad as might be supposed. Observations of the affairs of the Kung Bushmen of the Kalahari Desert in South Africa, for example, have yielded a great many surprises. Although the Kung live in a wasteland that no one else wants—a semidesert with only six to nine inches of rain per year—they seldom suffer from lack of food. Some 60 to 80 per cent of their diet is of vegetable origin. Their single most important foodstuff is the hard-shelled, protein-rich mongongo nut, the product of a drought-resistant tree, but the Bushmen also eat 84 other vegetables of varying attractiveness. During the comparatively rainy summer, January to March, they eat only the fruits, berries and melons they like best. During the dry season, May to October, they fall back on roots, shoots, bulbs and other less palatable, though no less nutritious, foods, especially after they have exhausted all the mongongo nuts within easy reach of water holes that have not yet gone dry. If really pressed, they can carry water with them on trips to draw on nut trees lying at a greater distance.

Nearly all the Kung's vegetable food is gathered by the women. The men may pick up a few nuts occasionally, but their normal job—when they feel like exerting themselves—is hunting. A few men do a great deal of this physically demanding work; others do little. The successful hunter earns prestige by bringing a lot of meat into camp, but he may not get much more meat to eat than anyone else. A traditional sharing system distributes it to everyone.

Anthropologist Richard B. Lee of the University of Toronto, who made an elaborate study of the Kung Bushmen a number of years ago, estimates that they eat on average 2,140 calories per day and 93.1 grams of protein, more than enough for such small people (Kung men average only five feet in height). The labour required to earn this ample diet is not great. No one works regular hours, but Lee estimates that a woman can gather enough food in one six-hour day to feed her family for three days. Men who really like to hunt or are eager to improve their social status by bringing back meat to vary the otherwise monotonous diet may spend a good deal of time searching for game, but the most enthusiastic hunter Lee encountered worked only 32 hours per week.

Many other nonagricultural tribes lead similarly easy lives, eating crudely but well and having plenty of time left over for dancing, religious rituals, ceremonial visits and sometimes less innocent pastimes such as gambling and warfare. There is no good reason to doubt that the ancient hunter-gatherers followed roughly the same pattern, with differences dictated by the regions in which they lived and the kinds of wild food available.

This ancient way of life, with its freedom, its leisure and its usually abundant supply of rough but nutritious food, seems attractive enough to make anthropologists wonder why it was ever abandoned by the hunter-gatherers of prehistoric times. There must have been compelling reasons to force men to take up the endless drudgery of farming.

Until fairly recently, most scholars agreed that the initial shift from foraging to farming was motivated by natural forces. A widely accepted theory, proposed in the 1930s by the British authority V. Gordon Childe, laid the change-over to a shift in climate at the end of the last ice age, around 10,000 B.C. According to Childe, fertile, well-watered areas thinly inhabited by hunter-gatherers dried up as the glaciers retreated. Many rivers stopped flowing. Deserts of shifting sand replaced forests and grasslands. In order to survive, the hunter-gatherers were forced to take refuge in a few remaining well-watered places, such as the Valley of the Nile in Egypt. Crammed together there, these refugees were stimulated by necessity to cultivate food-producing plants instead of relying on nature's limited bounty. They also fed and protected some of the wild animals driven into the oases by the scarcity of water elsewhere.

This theory was challenged in 1960 by Robert J. Braidwood of the University of Chicago, who pointed out in a paper based upon 10 years' work that the changes known to have taken place in the Middle Eastern climate were not nearly so drastic as Childe had assumed. Moreover, he argued, the transition to farming was less likely to have occurred in a crowded river valley or an oasis than in some other part of the Middle East where conditions were particularly favourable—where men and wild but domesticable plants and animals existed side by side. And since the earliest agricultural settlements then known—those of the Valley of the Nile, dating from around 4500 B.C.—were already fairly advanced, Braidwood conjectured that farming probably originated much earlier than anyone believed.

To test his theories, Braidwood planned an expedition that would be a departure from most previous ones to the Middle East. Earlier archaeologists, searching mainly for treasures with which to enrich the

Sparse vegetation, picked at by scattered sheep and goats, is all that remains of prehistoric agricultural efforts in an eroded, overgrazed region of

Iran. Here, in 6500 B.C., *the land supported not only herds of newly domesticated animals but also a variety of crops for the first farm families.*

18

Foothills of the Zagros Mountains are lush after spring rains in a climate largely unchanged since farming began here in 6500 B.C.

Tree-dotted slopes in Iran, rare survivors of overgrazing and deforestation, still look much as they did at the dawn of farming.

collections of sponsoring museums, had usually concerned themselves with some spectacular site such as the city of Ur of the Chaldees or the tomb of Tutankhamen. Braidwood intended instead to work towards the solution of a general problem—to fill what he considered a lamentable gap in man's knowledge of his past. Pointing out that the sequence of prehistoric development "seemed to jump from a late aspect of the cave stage immediately into the level of flourishing village-farming communities," he proposed to bridge this gap by finding a transitional village whose inhabitants straddled the borderline between hunting-gathering and farming.

Never did an archaeologist draw a truer aim. In choosing where to dig, Braidwood was guided by a knowledge of places where settlements on both sides of the archaeological gap had been found. He turned away from Childe's favoured Nile Valley and settled on what he called the hilly flanks of the Zagros Mountains in northeastern Iraq. "Within the hilly-flanks zone," he wrote, "occur in nature (or, in the case of some of the larger animals, occurred until recently) a remarkable constellation of the very plants and animals which became the basis for the food-producing pattern of the Western cultural tradition. Nowhere else in the world were the wild wheats and barley, the wild sheep, goats, pigs, cattle and horses to be found together in a single natural environment."

Since the climate of the Zagros region had been more or less the same many thousands of years ago as at present, the rainfall also would have been right —enough for incipient agriculture without irrigation, but not enough to encourage the growth of dense forests, which would have been a stumbling block to primitive farmers.

Like most inhabitable parts of the Middle East, northeastern Iraq is rich in traces of prehistoric life. Fragments of ancient clay vessels are scattered plentifully, and a skilled eye can tell at a glance whether the pot was broken by a medieval Moslem or by one of Darius' Persians in 500 B.C. In many places modern roads and fortifications have cut through layers of soil thick with the refuse and stone tools of long-forgotten peoples. The ancient past is everywhere waiting to tell its story.

The rolling hill country some 30 miles east of Kirkuk, 150 miles from Baghdad, which Braidwood selected for his dig, has suffered from thousands of years of careless cultivation and overgrazing. Today it is rather bare and desolate, but the young technique of palynology—the microscopic analysis of ancient pollen and other plant remains to determine what grew where in the past—has proved that from 10,000 to 7000 B.C. the area supported a few oaks interspersed with patches of grass and herbs. Hardly any trees grow there now, but the sod is not dense, and water is available in deeply cut watercourses called wadis that may stop running in summer but often have springs or water holes at the bottom.

Iraqi archaeologists had surveyed this country, which is now mostly grazing land, and briefly examined a place called Jarmo on a bend of the Cham-Gawra wadi. The site consisted of a low, rounded mound covering about three acres on a hilltop that may have offered advantages for defence, and it had the look of a spot that had been inhabited for a considerable time in the past. The undistinguished fragments of chipped or ground stone littering its surface were clearly not likely to attract an archaeologist searching for ancient splendours. Yet these apparently insignificant bits of stone were just the kind of evidence that Braidwood was looking for. They suggested to his trained eye that Jarmo might well date back to a time close to the dawn of agriculture.

A few preliminary trenches dug into the mound in 1948 were all that was needed to confirm Braidwood's suspicions, and he returned to Chicago to organize and finance a full-dress expedition. Two years later, accompanied by a team whose members included botanists, geologists and zoologists as well as archaeologists, he began serious digging.

Before long the low mound of Jarmo was yielding evidence that in its own way was as rewarding as the treasures of Tutankhamen or the rich royal burials found at Ur of the Chaldees. The mound consisted of a series of levels, or layers, each representing a settlement built upon the remains of a previous one. When Braidwood had dug down through these levels—some 16 in all—to the oldest, he discovered skeletal remains showing that the earliest inhabitants of Jarmo were not unlike the present Arab inhabitants of the area: a people of Mediterranean type, medium sized, probably with olive skin, dark eyes and dark hair. They lived in rectangular mud-walled houses of several rooms each, made surprisingly elegant cups and bowls of ground stone, fashioned human and animal figures of clay and wore bracelets and other ornaments of stone and bone. The presence of bones from onager, gazelle and other wild animals, plus shells from snails, acorns and pistachios, made it apparent that hunting-gathering supplied a substantial part of the diet.

A substantial part—but not all. The artifacts unearthed in the mound's lowest levels included not only mortars and pestles for grinding grain but also sickle blades of flint and obsidian and ground stone tools that may have been hoes—implements suggesting the cultivation of vegetable foods. Moreover, among the animal bones the expedition's zoologists identified those of goat and sheep that seem to have been domesticated: they were mature but small, as slaughtered domestic animals generally are.

But the proof that the first settlement at Jarmo was close to the borderline between hunting-gathering and a primitive kind of agriculture lay not in house construction, artifacts and animal bones but in still another discovery. Long-buried seeds showed that two kinds of cultivated wheat and one of barley—all of them close to wild forms but displaying kinship with today's domesticated varieties—were among the staples of the Jarmo food supply.

Only a few actual kernels of these grains were preserved inadvertently by their ancient cultivators. Since Jarmo was an open site exposed to the weather, rain water seeping through the soil would have caused plant materials to decay quickly. But some kernels had been subjected to heat in a conflagration or in an oven that charred them, without altering their form, in a way that prevented decay.

The prehistoric grains grown at Jarmo left other traces that Braidwood's botanist colleagues could read as clearly as print—impressions in the straw-tempered mud with which the villagers built their houses. The handiest place for the builders to get straw was probably a threshing floor where grain was separated from ears and stems brought in by the harvesters. Since the threshing process was primitive and imperfect, the chaffy material that collected around the floor contained a good many lost kernels, and these were kneaded with the straw into the mud for walls and house floors. The kernels themselves soon disintegrated, but the cavities that they left were imprints almost as detailed and informative as the original grain would have been. At Jarmo many clay floors and lower parts of walls were perfectly preserved, and much of the best information about the village's early crops was extracted from the imprints discovered in the mud construction materials.

At the end of four seasons of strenuous, painstaking digging, Braidwood and the members of his team added up the results of their work at Jarmo. The picture that emerged was very much like the imaginary scene that commenced this chapter—that of a small year-round village consisting of some two dozen mud houses inhabited by no more than 150 people. Unimpressive though Jarmo may have been as a settlement, it was, in Braidwood's words, "on the threshold of a new way of life". Here primitive farmers had been growing primitive wheat and barley as early as 7000 B.C., long before any kind of farming had been detected in Egypt.

Braidwood had made his point. He had not discovered the precise place or time of agriculture's origin—it must have taken a millennium or two before plant and animal domestication reached even such a primitive stage as Jarmo's. But the traces of farming Braidwood and his team unearthed on the hilly flanks of the Zagros Mountains were the oldest yet found. They also were far removed from any oasis surrounded by desert, so the Childe theory of climatic stress died—and remained dead.

What Braidwood had not felt it necessary to explain in much detail was what made the hunter-gatherers turn to the toilsome life of farmers. One theory, most forcefully presented by anthropologist

Kent V. Flannery of the University of Michigan, suggested that the ancient hunters of the Middle East (and very likely elsewhere also) passed through 10,000 years of "preadaptation", during which changes in their food supplies led to farming. After sifting through tons of debris from cave and outdoor living sites in a region stretching from Iraq's Zagros Mountains to the Taurus range in Turkey, Flannery and his colleagues concluded that about 20,000 B.C. the hunters who lived in the Taurus-Zagros region were being compelled by growing scarcities of accustomed foods to shift their diet.

Judging from bones and bone fragments in the deepest, oldest deposits, the meat that men had been eating since Homo erectus times had come almost entirely from large hoofed animals such as wild sheep, goats, cattle and pigs. The evidence of almonds, pistachios and other wild seeds indicated that the ancient hunter-gatherers ate a great deal of vegetable food as well, but they did not seem to bother much with small game.

The debris that came from slightly higher, younger deposits showed a gradual but significant shift away from the traditional large prey of the hunters. Hoofed animals still made the biggest contribution, but among them were traces of smaller, humbler creatures: turtles, land snails, fish, fresh-water crabs and molluscs, partridges and migratory water birds. It looked as if large animals could no longer supply all the people's protein needs, and the deficiency was being made good by foods that the proud hunters had formerly ignored.

Why did the food supply change? The reason could have been an increase of population that required a more intensive use of food resources. This ancient population crisis could have been brought about by reduction of one or more "antipopulation" factors. A very small change in living habits could have a big effect. A slight improvement in public hygiene, such as using latrines at a small distance from the centre of the camp, may have been enough to curtail a damaging disease or parasite. Or perhaps some change of custom, such as permitting widows to marry their late husbands' brothers, might have produced a few more children in each generation and so raised the population enough to put pressure on the supply of wild sheep and goats. Another possibility is that an improvement in weapons or hunting technique may have led to an increasing scarcity of game.

Whatever the cause, the hunting people of the Middle East gradually ceased to subsist mainly by killing large animals; instead they learned to exploit what Flannery calls a broad spectrum of animal and vegetable foods. This change made them familiar with all the sources and potential sources of food in their territory. And in those areas where certain foods were especially plentiful, they probably found it advantageous to concentrate on these resources and to remain near them.

Such specialized foragers could become more or less sedentary, exploiting one or a few foods intensively and wandering less in search of others. In the mountainous Taurus-Zagros region the foods that were particularly abundant included acorns and the seeds of various wild grasses, all of which needed processing to remove their shells or husks and make them edible. The abundance of these foods, too, may have encouraged permanent settlements, since processing involved the use of grinding stones and pots or other vessels for storage—equipment too heavy or too cumbersome to be carried about by seminomads.

There was one kind of grass, however, that yielded acceptable food without so great an investment of labour. It grew on mountain slopes, and its seeds clustered in two rows at the ends of slender stalks. They were quite large for grass seeds, nearly one-quarter of an inch long, and they had only thin, tightly clinging husks. They were the seeds of wild wheat—undoubtedly the most important plant in the history of Western civilization.

Until a few years ago, anthropologists interested in the economic underpinnings of the prehistoric Middle East debated rather academically about why wild wheat was the first plant to be domesticated in that region. One common assumption was that the women originally gathered the grain painfully stalk by stalk and made it a major part of the family diet only after they had learned to cultivate it artificially in solid stands. Another assumption was that the wild wheats (there are two closely related kinds) were greatly inferior to varieties that appeared after conscious farming was well underway.

The validity of both of these notions was undermined in 1966, when Jack R. Harlan, then a professor of agronomy at the University of Oklahoma, visited eastern Turkey. He was much impressed by dense and almost pure stands of ripe einkorn, one variety of wild wheat, growing on the rocky slopes of a volcanic mountain called Karacadag, and he wondered

An Iranian plateau exhibits three steps by which water aided farming in ancient times. At top, patches of ploughed land are watered chiefly by rain; because they are on a slope, they cannot be easily irrigated by the wadi or watercourse near by. At centre are fields which are watered by irrigation ditches. At bottom, a series of holes indicates a qanat— an underground aqueduct which taps subterranean water.

how attractive this food source would have been to ancient hunter-gatherers. He decided to try a practical experiment. First he stripped the grain and chaff from the stalks with his bare hands and stuffed it into a paper bag. His hands got raw in no time, but he found that he could pick an average of five and a half pounds per hour this way. When he used a 9,000-year-old flint sickle blade set in a new wooden handle to collect the einkorn, his rate went up to six and a quarter pounds per hour and his hands healed. He took his harvest back to the University of Oklahoma, had the chaff removed, and found that he had reaped more than two pounds of clean grain per hour. It was excellent grain, too, with 50 per cent more protein in it than in "hard red winter wheat", the modern grain grown in the Great Plains of the United States and Canada for bread flour.

The wild wheat fields of the hilly flanks began to look very good. Harlan calculated that on Karacadag during the three-week ripening season, a family of ancient reapers equipped with flint sickles or only their bare but callused hands could gather more grain than they could possibly eat in a year. No farming was necessary; the wild wheat grew of its own accord, as it still does where permitted to do so, from Israel north through Lebanon and Syria, west through eastern Turkey and southwest along the rugged mountains of Iraq and Iran.

Wherever the stands of wheat were good, bands of hunter-gatherers could have settled down close beside them, perhaps a few families in one place, a larger number in another. They would probably think of themselves as hunter-gatherers still, and the men would hunt whenever they could, but they would not dare leave unguarded the precious hoards of carefully protected grain. So they stayed close to their brimming granaries, and became villagers. They were not yet farmers, but they were the right people in the right place at the right time to make the crucial step. Within a few centuries they would no longer depend on collecting whatever nature provided; they would make nature give them what they needed.

The Benefits
—and Drawbacks—
of a Peaceful Revolution

At first glance there is nothing unusual about the scene at right; an old man's tale has simply attracted an attentive audience. Yet the painting, based on clues provided by excavations at prehistoric agricultural villages, sums up a profound revolution that was well underway in the Middle East by 7000 B.C. It shows a family, whose recent ancestors had been nomadic hunter-gatherers, settled in one place and leading the life of farmers.

Food raising (evidenced by the baby goat in a child's arms and the fields in the background) had begun to triumph over food collecting, and for good reason—it was clearly a more efficient way of life. While approximately 250 square miles of land were needed to feed a band of 25 foragers, six square miles could supply the 150 inhabitants of an early farming village with adequate food supplies. This productivity, which was increased still further by later improvements in agriculture, helped foster larger families, specialized labour and a variety of amenities.

The benefits of agriculture had particular meaning for old and young. Instead of being a burden to a band of roving foragers, an aged man like the one seen here could continue to serve as a memory bank of practical experience—a respected and needed member of the community. And children were valued for the contribution they could make to the family's well-being, as field hands and shepherds.

A farming family assembles to hear an elder impart the knowledge of his generation.

A Year-round Home Built with Straw, Mud and Teamwork

The busy scene at right, based in part on findings at the ancient site of Jarmo in the hills of Iraq, shows a farming family building a house about 8,500 years ago. The finished dwelling, like the two dozen others that make up their village, will be small and simple, largely because the farmers lack the tools to build anything more advanced. The chief construction material they use is *tauf*, a coarse mixture of mud and straw, applied in layers and baked hard by the sun. Although vulnerable to winter rains, the house qualifies as a permanent dwelling. Moreover, this type of building was one of the earliest constructed for year-round habitation by man.

The house was planned to provide the family of 10 with adequate living space (the larger room is 18 feet long), storage areas and a courtyard. The task of building it involved many days of co-ordinated labour by every adult member of the family. After stones were put in place for the foundation, work began on the six-foot-high walls, which were built up of *tauf* in thin layers of diminishing width, with about a day of drying time allowed between each new layer.

Here, as the family's long labour on their house nears completion, poles laid from wall to facing wall are covered over with branches, then with straw and twigs. Finally a thick coat of mud is spread on by hand to form a substantial roof.

Seven family members labour in teams to complete a typical early house. Workers at top right and

wer left trample mud and straw and carry the mixture in baskets to a wall-builder and two roofers, who use it to coat thatching laid on top of beams.

The Kitchen: Centre of a New Technology

Beneath some 7,500 years of detritus, excavators at Tell Hassuna, in Iraq, uncovered a farming village whose kitchens consisted of two cooking areas, as in the painting at right. In the hot, dry months, the women prepared and cooked food in airy courtyards equipped with hearths and, in some cases, ovens. But in variable weather they worked comfortably around indoor hearths, perhaps venturing out to bake loaves of unleavened bread.

Kitchens such as this one were in many ways the focal point of the agricultural revolution. The foods processed in them represented a radical change in diet, with wheat and barley replacing game and other wild foods as the mainstay. Fired vessels of pottery—too cumbersome and fragile for hunter-gatherers to carry in their wanderings—served as durable containers for cooking or storing foods and liquids. Such wares enabled cooks to prepare or preserve the harvested grains by boiling, parching, germinating or fermenting them.

Thanks to these innovations, women like the four in the picture could put together meals that were varied, if not particularly exciting. The main course, served with the bread, was likely to be a porridge, possibly flavoured with chunks of game. For the dessert, there might be nuts or fruit. All this was probably washed down with copious draughts of a heady new beverage: barley beer.

Four women prepare dinner for their large family. Their tasks involve stirring a meaty porridge in a

ot over a fire, placing flat bread in the outdoor oven, grinding grain scooped from a sunken bin, and dipping water out of a large pottery jar.

In a workshop building, a craftsman cuts a thin bone into beads behind a display of his wares, while the worker in the next stall polishes

Spare Time for Craftsmen to Work in Bone and Stone

bone spatula. Outside, a woman tries on an antelope-bone necklace while a craftsman strings another.

As the farmers became more efficient, they found themselves—especially in the off-season between crops—with a bonus of spare time that they could use to fashion the workaday articles they needed. And some eventually were to discover—perhaps to their surprise—that they could even make part of their living as craftsmen.

In the village of Beidha, in Jordan, craftsmen appeared as early as 6500 B.C. Their workshops were clustered in and around a number of arcade-like buildings, one of which is reconstructed here. The building consisted of a 20-foot-long corridor, which gave access to six small workshops arranged in facing pairs. The structure's fitted-stone exterior and the massive walls separating the shops apparently supported a second-story living area.

In one workshop, excavators unearthed heavy stone cutting tools and animal skeletons that suggested its occupant had been a butcher. But such a high degree of specialization was rare in this early period. Far more common were craftsmen who made particular wares in different materials or general wares in one material. A man who worked in bone would produce necklaces, pins, bracelets and even shovels—the latter made of an aurochs' shoulder blade. An experienced stoneworker would make a great variety of implements, such as axeheads, blades and scrapers, grinding stones, mortars and pestles.

Perils and Portents of the Farming Life

Fleeing a fire with all the valuables that they can carry, members of a farming family (left) abandon their village house to flames, which hav

With its varied benefits, agriculture brought a host of new problems. The work of farming was not only harder than foraging, it was riskier as well: crop failures could lead to famines or malnutrition. In addition, an advantage of the sedentary life—the accumulation of material possessions—could be a drawback, especially if fire engulfed the straw-roofed village. The greatest tragedy was the burning of hoarded grain supplies.

Reverses such as these taught the farmers how to adapt and plan ahead. They learned, for example, to feed part of their grain surpluses to their sheep and goats when browse was limited—thus ensuring healthy animals for supplementary food. But the expanding village populations were unprepared for the long-range effects that agriculture would have on the land. In many large areas, intensive farming crowded out game and natural vegetation. Hunting and gathering, man's way of life for over a million years, was nearing its end.

already spread to a neighbour's tinder-dry straw roof. There one man struggles to smother the sparks while two others rescue an elderly cripple.

How did the first farmers learn to farm? This question has fascinated men of learning (and many without learning) since earliest times, and innumerable answers have been proposed, ranging from the decorative myths of antiquity to increasingly informed guesses by modern scholars.

According to the ancient Egyptians, all men were cannibals until the great god Osiris instructed them in the art of planting and showed them how to make agricultural tools. The Greek credited the birth of farming to their goddess Demeter; they believed that she gave wheat seeds to her priest, Triptolemus, and instructed him to drive around the earth in his chariot drawn by dragons and serpents, bringing the blessings of agriculture and civilization to all men. When the Romans took over and renamed many of the Greek gods and goddesses, Demeter became Ceres, from whom the word cereal (meaning grain in general) is derived.

Belief in a legendary or mythological origin of farming has long been out of fashion, but even today the question of how men became food producers instead of merely food gatherers cannot be answered precisely, and the exact steps by which they did so are likely to remain hidden in the remote past. What can be said with reasonable certainty, however, is that the steps were first taken in the Middle East, where traces of plant cultivation are the oldest known, dating back at least 9,000 years. Moreover, the

A clay statuette, found on the island of Cyprus, portrays a timeless chore: a woman grinds threshed grain on a stone while her daughter shakes the product in a sieve, sifting out the coarser bits and storing the flour in a jar in the foreground. The use of stones to grind grain dates back over 10,000 years and persisted on Cyprus into the 20th Century.

evidence unearthed there to date indicates that farming originated in a region where the wild prototypes of wheat and barley were sufficiently abundant to tempt bands of nomadic hunter-gatherers to settle in the neighbourhood and make their meals mainly of the easily collected seeds.

But while the events that led to the domestication of these plants may never be known with exactness, a mounting number of clues, pieced together by painstaking archaeological detective work, have produced some intriguing knowledge of how farming probably came about.

A large part of the knowledge stems from the work of scientists who specialize in studying the plant remains of ancient cultures and who are known by the formidable title of palaeoethnobotanists. Among their most valuable clues for reconstructing the birth of farming in the Middle East are the remains of ancient seeds or other vegetable matter, such as the charred wheat and barley grains found by Robert Braidwood when he excavated the 9,000-year-old village of Jarmo in northeastern Iraq. These black carbonized survivors from the distant past can be fairly reliably dated by the carbon-14 method, which measures the extent of radiocarbon decay in organic matter. Charred seeds are not uncommon in early dwelling sites, where indoor cooking fires under low thatched roofs made huts burn down frequently. In some of these conflagrations, wheat kernels on the floors or in storage receptacles got covered in such a way that they were protected from oxygen while being heated and charred. Even when the house did not catch fire, wheat was often carbonized in the hot wood ashes of indoor hearths. Neolithic housewives were not notable for their neatness, but the sloppiest of them apparently swept their clay floors once in a while, and often the litter containing spilled wheat grains went into the smouldering fireplace. The nature of wild and early cultivated wheats also led to some carbonized grains. The kernels of these cereals were enclosed in tight-fitting protective husks that had to be loosened by heating. Sometimes a housewife let the heating go too far and blackened the family dinner. The inedible kernels would be discarded, to be found by archaeologists thousands of years after the careless housewife had dried her tears.

Even when grains of wheat did not become carbonized, they sometimes left other telltale traces: detailed impressions of their shape, which were preserved in mud mixed with straw like that used by the Jarmo villagers to build their houses. The clay of coarse pottery also was frequently mixed with straw that acted as a binder and kept the vessel from cracking while drying in the sun. When the clay was fired it turned to hard, bricklike matter that would last almost forever, immortalizing any embedded wheat grains as burned-out impressions.

A more subtle clue shedding light on the plants of the earliest farmers is the silica skeleton left in ancient refuse pits or wherever vegetable matter has decayed. When sap rises in living plants it normally contains a small amount of dissolved silica. It is in a sense the plant's excretion; the plant does not need this inert material and gets rid of it as silica, which is deposited as lacy skeletons on its leaves and stems. These delicate patterns remain after the rest of the plant has disappeared. Thousands of years later, under the palaeoethnobotanist's microscope, they reveal not only what kind of plant they came from but even what part of that plant.

The silica that formed on the leaves and stems of long-dead plants is also revealing in a more obvious way. Silica is highly abrasive, so when an archaeologist turns up a flint blade or other sharp tool showing the characteristic sheen imparted by silica, he can tell that it was used for harvesting grain instead of for cutting meat or hides.

Often the seeds and other informative organic remains found on a site are mixed with large amounts of soil and other mineral matter. Searching through this mixture by hand is tedious and ineffective, so up-to-date archaeologists use a process known as flotation. One kind of flotation is to simply put a sample of soil from an excavation into a tub with water and gently slosh it around. The mineral matter, being heavier than the organic material, sinks quickly, allowing any plant remains and bone fragments present to rise to the surface and be scooped up.

A fancier kind of flotation—froth flotation—was originally developed by the mining industry to separate fine particles of ore from worthless dross. Froth flotation depends on the fact that some substances stick to each other while others do not. If certain oily liquids, called collectors, are mixed with a mud solution containing organic particles such as carbonized seeds, they coat the seeds but do not coat sand, clay or other mineral matter. In this oil-covered state the organic particles have become aerophilic (attracted to air), while the rest of the mixture remains hydrophilic (attracted to water).

The archaeological use of this principle is simple. A cylindrical container is filled with water to which is added a few teaspoons of kerosene. A detergent is also added to emulsify the kerosene and form a long-lasting froth. The material to be separated is carefully screened to remove large objects and poured slowly into the container while compressed air is forced through a perforated ring of pipe in the container's bottom. Fine bubbles rising to the top carry with them the aerophilic organic particles, while the hydrophilic mineral particles sink towards the bottom. Thus the froth, when skimmed off the surface, contains only the carbonized seeds and any other organic matter of possible archaeological value.

But once an ancient site has yielded primitive wheat—in carbonized form, as impressions in mud or pottery or as silica skeletons—there is still an unanswered question: how to tell from such traces whether the wheat was wild or cultivated? "Easy," say the palaeoethnobotanists. The two kinds of wild wheat that grew in the Middle East 10,000 years ago are still found growing there today. Their names are wild einkorn (*Triticum boeoticum*) and wild emmer (*Triticum dicoccoides*). They are very much like the primitive domesticated einkorn and emmer, but they differ slightly in the size and shape of their kernels and in other small but revealing details. An expert has little trouble distinguishing the wild and the domesticated variety, even though the specimen may be thousands of years old. But there is still another difference between cultivated einkorn and emmer and their wild ancestors—a difference that was vastly important for the birth of farming.

As the kernel-bearing ears of wild einkorn and emmer ripen, they "shatter", the kernels at the tips breaking away first, followed by the others until all are gone. When an ear is in this fragile condition, the touch of a harvester's hand or cutting tool is apt to make many of the kernels fall to the ground, where they are lost. In contrast, the ears of cultivated wheat

tend to hold together until they can be gathered whole at the harvester's leisure.

From the wild wheat's point of view, fragility is beneficial. Wheat is an annual plant that dies each year and depends on its seeds to continue its species. It grows best in a climate that has temperate, rainy winters and hot, dry summers, and its natural habitat is bare or recently disturbed soil: rocky hillsides that offer soil-filled crannies between the rocks, on steep stream banks where the ground has slumped, in dirt scuffed by animals, or in any other patches of soil not tightly occupied by established vegetation. To exploit such opportunities, the wild wheat produces in early summer an unusually large seed, the wheat kernel, that will stay dormant during the dry season and promptly start vigorous growth when the autumn rains begin.

To make sure the heavy seeds have a chance to get a good start in receptive soil, nature has provided a wild wheat like emmer with an ingenious planting mechanism (*pages 40-41*). Each seed is part of a spikelet, a chaffy husk that has a sharp point at the base, a lot of short hairs slanting away from the point and long, stiff, bristle-like "awns" at the other end. As the ear of wheat ripens, the spikelets begin to break away. Strong winds often carry them a considerable distance from the parent plant. When one of these spikelets falls towards the earth, the aerodynamic drag of the long awns makes it behave like a dart. It hits the ground with its tapered base forward, and if the soil is fairly soft and loose the sharp point penetrates it. Then the backward-pointing hairs cause the capsule containing the seed to dig itself gradually into the ground. This self-planting process is remarkably efficient. A few weeks after its seeds have ripened, a

Turned to carbon by intense heat and thus preserved for
thousands of years, kernels of einkorn wheat display
the differences that enable archaeologists to tell the wild type
(upper picture) from domesticated wheat (lower picture).
Shown enlarged roughly four times, the wild grains from a
site in Syria are small and slender; domestication has bred
the others, excavated in Greece, to a larger, fatter shape.

stand of wild wheat shows nothing but bare stalks and the long awns of the spikelets sticking out of the soil. The hidden, hard-husked seeds are reasonably safe from the voracious appetites of birds, rodents and insects and are ready to start into rapid growth as soon as enough rain has fallen.

However advantageous for the wild-wheat plant, this seed-dissemination system was tough on prehistoric wheat gatherers. The ears ripened over a three-week season, and the picker often obtained immature grain of low quality or saw ripe ears shatter before she (doubtless most wheat gatherers were women) had a chance to tuck them safely into her basket. How often she must have climbed a slope to a thriving wheat patch only to find most of the golden grain already blown away by the wind or waiting to shatter at a touch of her flint-bladed sickle. How often she must have pestered her gods for wheat that did not behave like that.

In a sense the gods had already responded. Like most wild species, wild wheat is variable. A few of its plants have genetic peculiarities and produce ears that appear normal but do not shatter. The spikelets of this kind of wheat have tough stems that hold them to the stalk long after normal spikelets have flown away on the wind. This trait is disadvantageous in wild wheat; such aberrant plants are doomed to have few if any descendants because not enough of their seeds break away to distribute and plant themselves. To human harvesters, on the other hand, this characteristic is an advantage; the freak plants are ideal because their nonshattering ears can be gathered over a longer period.

Modern myth-makers sometimes spin a pleasant tale about how, around 7000 B.C., an extra-bright girl may have noticed this unusual kind of wild wheat. She collected a basketful of nonshattering ears and planted their seeds near her village. The crop they produced next season was all nonshattering, and it became the base of the farming way of life. But palaeoethnobotanists do not think that any bright girl was needed. They point out that nonshattering wheat ears would naturally form a disproportionately large part of the harvest brought back to the village, since they could be cut without losing any grains. Towards the end of the ripening season they would be the only ears left, and women and children no doubt shouldered their baskets and made special trips to gather them from distant wheat patches that they had not had time to visit sooner. During this late season they would have returned with their baskets filled almost entirely with nonshattering ears.

The untidy habits of prehistoric villagers made certain that many wheat grains would be spilled or otherwise lost near the village where some would find exactly what was needed for successful growth next season. All primitive habitations are surrounded by various kinds of bare or disturbed soil: footpaths, animal footprints, fallen mud buildings, refuse dumps, latrines, dance floors of beaten earth, the sites of old outdoor fires. All these would offer spots where spilled wheat could get a foothold. Since the greater part of the wheat brought to the village was the nonshattering kind, an abnormal number of the plants springing up on its dumps and along its paths would be nonshattering too. Most villages were built on relatively level spots handy to water, but often at a considerable distance from the scattered stands of wild wheat. When the villagers found patches of superior wheat springing up in their immediate neigh-

A Wild Grass That Changed the World

The notion that anatomy is destiny can apply not only to humans but also to an important plant like wheat. Wild emmer—one of the ancestors of today's wheats—was harvested by hunter-gatherers at least as far back as 10,000 B.C. in the Middle East. But like all wild grasses, it possessed a trait annoying to harvesters employing primitive sickles: the seed-bearing ear, or spike, shattered as soon as it was ripe. This mechanism allowed emmer to seed itself. But some emmer had tougher spikes that did not fall apart when the stems were cut, and apparently more of this type was brought back home by harvesters. There, whether intentionally planted or simply spilled on the ground, it began to predominate and eventually became domesticated wheat.

Nearly all of its other characteristics, however, remained the same as those of the easily shattered wild wheat. It retained such primitive self-propagating devices as the long, stiff bristles, called awns or beards, that caught and travelled in the fur of animals or blew about on strong winds, and the small, spiky hairs along the base of the kernels that allowed emmer to anchor itself in the ground. It also kept the hard outer husks that made freeing the edible kernels inside such difficult work for the first farmers, as the drawings in the bottom row at right demonstrate.

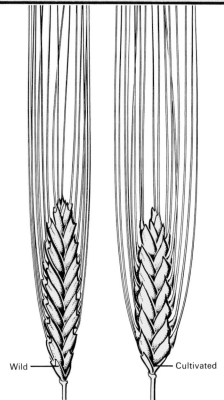

Wild — Cultivated

Emmer Wheat Spike

The drawings above show a spike of wild emmer and of cultivated emmer. The spike in the wild variety usually measures about three inches long, and slightly less in the cultivated form. The grains of wild emmer are smaller and less densely packed than those of the domesticated type. In harvesting emmer, the farmers cut the spikes from the stems, as shown below, with wooden or bone sickles into which sharp-edged bits of flint were set.

Harvesting

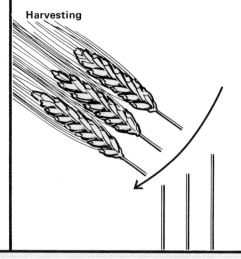

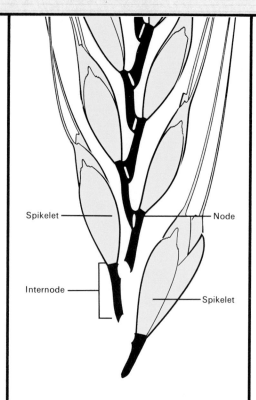

Spikelet — Node

Internode — Spikelet

The Spike Diagrammed

A drawing of an emmer spike shows the axis, or rachis, and how it is jointed. The joints are called nodes and the segments between them internodes. At maturity wild emmer comes apart at the nodes, while in the cultivated emmer the spikelets remain intact. Breaking up the rachis to separate the spikelets required threshing. The farmers did this by flailing the spikes with long sticks until the spikelets broke away, as indicated below.

Threshing

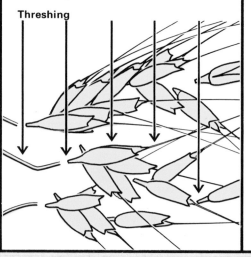

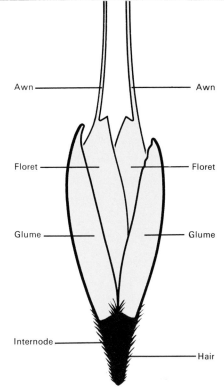

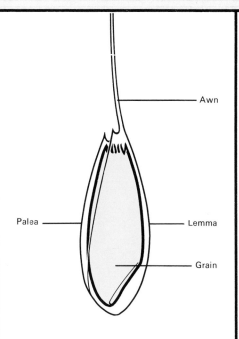

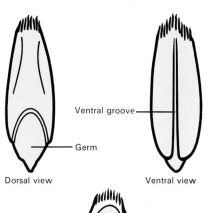

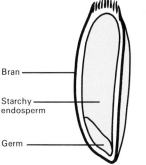

Longitudinal section

The Spikelet

An emmer spikelet is a study in nature's adaptability. It consists of two outer husks, or glumes, enclosing two florets, each of which has a wirelike awn and contains a grain. The base, or internode, is covered with small, tough, backward-pointing hairs that helped wild wheat to dig itself into the ground. To free the spikelets from the chaff, the farmers winnowed the wheat by tossing it high in the air and letting the lighter straw blow away.

The Floret

The protective covering of the floret made extra work for the early farmer. The floret consists of two inner glumes, the lemma and palea, which tightly enclose the grain. To free the grain from both the inner and outer glumes, pounding was required —perhaps preceded by parching to make the glumes brittle. The pounding was probably done with mortar and pestle (below). Today's wheats have loose glumes that threshing removes.

The Grain

The dorsal surface of an emmer grain (above, left) is rounded, while the ventral side (right) has a deep groove. The grain itself, as shown in the longitudinal section at centre, is composed of the protein-rich germ, the bran and the starchy endosperm. To get rid of the glumes, the farmers winnowed the wheat again (below), and then may have ground the grain for breadmaking, or cooked the cracked kernels into a porridge.

Winnowing

Pounding

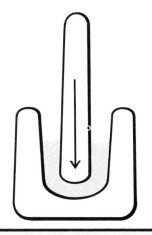

Winnowing

bourhood, they no doubt credited their gods with a benevolent miracle.

This partial domestication of wheat—or perhaps it should be called self-domestication—is now known to have happened in various parts of the Middle East by 7000 B.C. But partial domestication probably did not take place in all settlements of wheat gatherers. The soil, rainfall and other local conditions would have had to be especially favourable, and a village would have had to exist in the same location for a considerable time.

So the next and crucial step towards true farming must have occurred: saving seed and planting it deliberately. Wherever this step was first taken, it is likely to have been preceded by earnest debates in the villages about what could be done to encourage more grain to grow near by. Gods or goddesses in charge of fertility were petitioned, sacrifices offered, diviners consulted.

That seeds can grow into green plants was probably known, at least in a vague sort of way, before agriculture developed. Certainly the gatherers of wild wheat must have noticed how green sprouts appeared when their stored grain got thoroughly rain-soaked and was not promptly spread in the sun to dry. But using this knowledge practically was quite another matter. It may not have been applied until an increase in the population or a need for grain to trade for meat or other desirables such as flint for tools made deliberate planting imperative.

Deliberate planting could have come about in any number of ways. Perhaps grain was considered sacred and was scattered as an offering on the ground near some holy spot. If so, the worshippers may have noticed that it reproduced its kind. Less romantically,

Basic Equipment for Early Cooks

A pottery milk jug, with lip and painted design

A ceramic husking tray, its bottom grooved for stripping grain

A stone pot, asymmetrical but finely made

A ceramic ladle with a primitive handle

A heavy stone quern and round pestle, used for grinding husked grain

Fashioned in Iraq between 7000 and 4000 B.C., the kitchen equipment shown here sums up an age of changing life styles. The quern and grinding stone above—too heavy for hunter-gatherers to carry from camp to camp—typify the crude early implements made by farmers living in one place. The cooking pot next to it represents a later refinement: finely ground stone vessels. Such vessels were eventually replaced by more easily made pottery like the husking tray and milk jug at left.

some villager may have remarked that wheat was apt to appear of its own accord near a threshing floor, so he moved his floor each year to encourage new wheat patches. Or a woman may have accidentally spilled a basket of threshed wheat on a refuse dump and not retrieved it all. When a dense growth of wheat plants appeared at that spot, she may have been inspired to sow the whole dump with wheat. And, of course, there may really have been foresighted persons who made observations, formed the proper conclusion from the evidence and planted wheat seeds in well-prepared ground.

It is not likely that the new technique of seed planting was discovered in a single village and then swept quickly through the wild-wheat belt of the Middle East. In those dim years 100 centuries ago, the villages of grain gatherers must have kept pretty much to themselves. Not only were they widely separated, but they probably spoke dialects that only a few neighbours could understand, had different customs, worshipped different gods and perhaps were even belligerent about it. They might have done a little trading in much-desired goods such as decorative sea shells and obsidian for razor-sharp knives or sickle blades, but otherwise most of the villages were probably grimly hostile to each other, regarding any outsider as a potential threat to their precious stands of wild wheat. Under these conditions the new technique could not have spread very fast.

The judgment of both anthropologists and palaeo-ethnobotanists is that the practice of planting seed in prepared ground was adopted independently many times and at different places in the Middle East, beginning around 8000 B.C., but always near habitats where wild grain grew naturally. In some villages the

The Important Invention of the Oven

One of the most significant benefits derived from farming's settled life was the oven, three basic types of which are diagrammed here. Built of clay, each was used primarily for baking bread—the flat loaves adhered to the heated sides. The oven was also the predecessor of the kiln and the smelting furnace.

Two of the early ovens (above) were similar in design but differently insulated. The subterranean one used the surrounding earth; the one at right had a lining of pebbles and mud between layers of clay. Both types burned wood on a bed of stones.

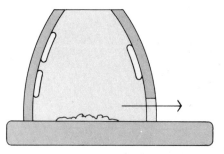

A more advanced oven, two to three feet high, had several improvements over the smaller types at top. This one was built on a heat-conserving clay base; also, its narrow opening and small side vent (arrow) created a draught that produced a hotter fire.

first crop may have been barley, which behaves very much like wheat, and other crops, such as peas and lentils, soon became important. The old-fashioned gathering way of life usually continued while cultivation was being developed. In what is now Syria and Israel, especially at the northern end of the Jordan Valley, wild wheat seems to have grown so abundantly that surprisingly elaborate and populous settlements were supported by gathering alone. But in the less favoured regions the settlers were forced to develop cultivation.

While full credit goes to the prehistoric villagers who domesticated wheat and barley, the effectiveness of these plants in getting themselves domesticated should not be overlooked. Their wild forms have a very limited range: mostly small zones and patches in the Middle East. They first attracted man's attention by their large, edible seeds and then offered occasional nonshattering ears that, though suicidal in the wild state, were perfect for man to adopt as a cultivated crop. Thus, in these areas wheat, barley and man became contented symbionts, and man has since spread the domesticated seeds to all temperate parts of the earth.

Because farming enabled—and, to an extent, forced—man to move, it is unlikely that the early farmers willingly left their cosy villages where wheat grew of its own accord, or with only a little help, to move into places where it had to be planted. Most anthropologists now believe that some of them were forced to move by demographic pressure, an increase in population made possible by the prosperity and cultural growth resulting from settled life and a handy food supply. Settled folk would have fewer hunting accidents than wandering hunter-gatherers,

and predation (children getting eaten by lions) would be less common. Probably even more important would be a decline of infanticide. The women of nomadic hunters were compelled to dispose of infants whom they could not carry on a long march. The women of permanent settlements made no such marches, and presumably tried to raise all of their children, even when food was scarce. Nor did other helpless or near-helpless individuals—the cripples and the sick and the old—have to be abandoned as often as in the case of nomads. Their survival would also play a part in increasing the population, and as the cultural level gradually rose the village elders became valuable as the possessors of special skills and as repositories of experience and tradition.

Eventually, in village after village the supply of wheat and of cultivable land must have fallen behind the demands of the expanding population. So daughter colonies budded off, some moving to places where wheat did not grow naturally. Some of these colonists may have experimented a few years earlier to find ground suitable for wheat. When they found a favourable site for their settlement, they may have departed in peace, or even with help from the parent village. Or perhaps a religious leader (for religion is far older than agriculture) led a group of his followers into the wilderness like Brigham Young taking the Mormons to Utah.

Other buddings-off were not so peaceful. Large villages undoubtedly encroached on smaller ones, first barring their harvesters from their outlying wildwheat fields, then from their planted patches. Then the village itself might be attacked and all except the younger women killed or driven away. In other cases a village that had grown too big for its food supply, both wild and cultivated, may have divided into hostile factions, one of which was forced to leave.

In all cases except the most hurried flights, the departing colonists presumably took with them, in baskets or leather pouches, the best wheat seeds that they could get their hands on, and the women at least would know that the nonshattering kind was best for harvesting. So the crops they planted and gathered in their new home were almost entirely the domesticated, nonshattering type.

The new wheat and barley proved remarkably adaptable to their new conditions. When planted in properly loosened soil at the proper season, they produced better crops than their wild ancestors, which had to contend with rocks, competing vegetation and the grazing of wild animals. Preparing the soil was laborious. The first tilling was probably accomplished with nothing more elaborate than a sharp-pointed digging stick. More efficient tools were not needed. When wheat is eaten directly by the family that grows it, not much land need be tilled. Even if the yield were as poor as 10 bushels per acre, two acres would provide the basic food for a family.

Now, possessing both domesticated grain and knowledge of tilling, the Middle Easterners could for the first time be called true farmers—and could move on to other areas. Slowly the belt of cultivation spread to all but the most unfavourable lands of the Middle East. In some places the first dozen (or hundred) harvests may have been poor, but the natural variability of wheat and barley came to the rescue. If rain was deficient in a newly settled region, the wheat plants that needed the most moisture would be stunted and yield little or no seeds. They would not be as well represented in the next crop that the farmer planted, so gradually the local strain became drought-resistant. Other strains developed resistance to cold and unseasonable wetness. Eventually wheat was able to thrive and could be carried anywhere its human symbionts wanted to take it.

Everyday Staples from Prehistory's Larder

Many of the plants that the farmers learned to grow thousands of years ago are today so much a part of nearly everyone's diet that it is difficult to think of their being gathered by hand in the wild. And so common are they that their origins in diverse parts of the globe often go overlooked.

Domestication occurred not only in the Middle East, where wheat and barley were the first of man's crops, but in East Asia and the New World as well. East Asia, for example, contributed the foods depicted at left, including such staples as rice, soya beans and sugar cane. Farmers in China were growing millet (a grain still eaten by one-third of the world's population) as early as 4500 B.C., about a millennium earlier than rice, which was to become their most well-known crop.

By 3000 B.C. soya beans had become a regular part of the Oriental diet; their importance as a source of cheap protein is well recognized today. Scientists forecast the eventual use of these nutritious beans as a meat substitute around the world.

1. Adsuki beans
2. Yellow bananas
3. Red bananas
4. Green bananas
5. Soya beans
6. Coconuts
7. Millet
8. Yams
9. Sugar cane
10. Rice

A Cornucopia of Foodstuffs from the Middle East

Were it not for the Middle East, where wheat was first domesticated and still grows wild, there would be no bread —at least the bread most people know. Besides being the world's first breadbasket, the Middle East contributed many other important foods, including those shown at right. In the millennia after 8000 B.C., farmers added to their crops of wheat and barley a variety of legumes, including chickpeas, lentils and fava beans. Such foods were extremely practical; they could be eaten fresh when they were in season, or dried and stored.

In the centuries that followed 4000 B.C., some of the Middle Eastern farmers turned their skills to raising products that enlivened and enriched their diet—figs and apricots, almonds and pistachios, walnuts and dates, olives and grapes. From olives came oil not only for cooking but also for lamps. And the grape, when pressed, yielded juice that could be fermented to make wine, a beverage that added a whole new dimension of pleasure to life.

1. Lentils
2. Chick-peas
3. Salt
4. Peas
5. Raisins
6. Olives
7. Barley
8. Walnuts
9. Almonds
10. Pistachio nuts
11. Apricots
12. Dates
13. Wheat
14. Figs
15. Fava beans

Rich and Colourful Gifts from the Americas

When New World farmers began to domesticate the edible wild plants they found around them, they could hardly have imagined the impact these foods—some of which are shown here—would one day have on the world. The potato, first grown in the Andes around 2000 B.C., would help save Europeans from famine; corn would stave off the hunger of America's first settlers; and beans would add both protein and variety to the diets of hungry people everywhere.

The whole great adventure of agriculture in Latin America dates back to about 7000 B.C., when farmers in Mexico and Peru first began to grow such foods as bottle gourds and avocados. By 6000 B.C. beans were being raised and one thousand years later, squash. Both were prized for their flesh and their nutritious seeds. Corn, cultivated since at least 5500 B.C., became Mexico's major crop around 1500 B.C. These staples were enlivened by such foods as the chilli pepper and cocoa bean. Combined, chilli and chocolate made a pungent drink enjoyed by ancient Mexicans.

1. Pink beans
2. Lima beans
3. Manioc
4. White potatoes
5. Summer squash
6. Acorn squash
7. Small dried chillies
8. Fresh chillies
9. Corn cob
10. Dried chillies
11. Cocoa beans
12. Whole dried corn
13. Cracked dried corn
14. Pinto beans
15. Shelled pumpkin seeds

While farming was slowly spreading from the Middle East, where it had originated around 8000 B.C., it was also sprouting independently in other parts of the ancient world. During the next 4,000 years, in areas as widely separated as South America and China, people were learning to cultivate different plants native to their regions. And like wheat, which today is a basic food for nearly half of the earth's inhabitants, some of the other plants developed in these lands eventually produced staples or favoured items for man's diet around the globe.

Corn, white potatoes, peanuts, avocados, tomatoes and squashes—to name only a few of the dozen or more foods first grown by the Indians of prehistoric America—now help to feed many of the temperate and semitropical areas of both the Old World and the New. Rice, sugar cane, yams, bananas and other plants first cultivated in China or Southeast Asia thousands of years ago now grow in virtually all moist, tropical regions.

Thus, although the earliest evidences of farming have come from the Middle East, there were "first" farmers in other parts of the world, especially in East Asia and Central and South America. Farming was, in fact, born several times over in different areas and at different times. And one of its earliest and most important birthplaces was China.

In China, odd as it might seem, the first plant to be domesticated was not the one most associated with

A group of young men and women propitiate Chicomecoatl, the Aztec goddess of corn, with cornstalks and bowls of gruel. This illustration is one of many collected from the Indians by Friar Bernardino de Sahagun, who came to Mexico in 1529 and travelled extensively to gather information about agriculturally based religious ceremonies of the Aztecs.

the area—rice—but a grass called millet which, in the United States today, is usually sold as birdseed. A tall grass that produces fuzzy seed heads resembling caterpillars, millet provided the base for China's ancient civilization. This plant is still grown in northern China where it evolved; cultivated varieties have spread to India, Japan, Indonesia, North Africa and Europe. Despite its limited use in the United States, millet continues to be eaten by nearly a third of the world's population.

The place where millet was domesticated, sometime before 4000 B.C., was quite different from the moist and fertile plains near the mouths of the Yellow and Yangtze rivers that now support the greater part of China's population. The original seedbed is a rather forbidding region located on the middle reaches of the river Yellow. The climate there is bitterly cold in winter and the rainfall is scant, ranging from 10 to 20 inches per year.

Though there are much pleasanter places in China, this Nuclear Area, as the archaeologists call it, had definite advantages. It was free of the dense forests and the heavy, perennial sod that might have discouraged people equipped only with primitive tools. Moreover, the soil there is of a variety called loess, a fine-grained yellowish loam so soft and porous that it can be cultivated with the simplest digging sticks. It does not lose its fertility quickly, as forest and tropical soils are likely to do.

There is a drawback to loess as well. It also erodes easily and imparts its colour to the river Yellow and the Yellow Sea into which the river pours, but in 4000 B.C., with the land only beginning to be cultivated, erosion was not yet a problem in northern China.

Chinese literature and legend point to the loess

country as the birthplace of the Chinese people themselves. But the region's harsh climate made it seem so unfavourable as a cradle of humanity that many scholars discounted its importance until the 1930s. That was when Chinese archaeologists excavated an important city in northern Honan Province. It turned out to be An-yang, the legendary capital of the Shang Dynasty that flourished between 1600 and 1100 B.C. And the relics of An-yang indicated that if the loess country had indeed been the birthplace of the Chinese people and their extraordinary culture, its inhabitants had come a long way by Shang times.

An-yang was no primitive collection of crude huts, but a splendid metropolis with spectacular bronze-work, horse-drawn war chariots and even inscriptions representing the beginnings of Chinese writing. Moreover, the discovery of stone hoes, spades and sickles—and ditches that may have been used for irrigating fields—showed that Shang agricultural techniques were well developed.

But was there proof of much earlier beginnings of Chinese agriculture? Some archaeologists suspected that An-yang and the Shang culture might be a transplant, brought in from the Middle East. They offered as evidence the Shang custom of burying their rulers with quantities of elegant grave goods and hundreds of human victims sacrificed to serve them in the other world. The same gruesome funerary rite was a custom in ancient Mesopotamia about 3,800 miles to the west. This and similar bits of evidence suggested that the Shang civilization may have arrived full blown from the Middle East. If so, An-yang's agriculture could have been imported too.

But archaeologists soon proved that Chinese agriculture was no import. Further excavations uncov-

ered other Chinese towns and villages, which were carbon-dated back to 4000 B.C., more than 2,000 years before the rise of the Shang civilization. These earlier settlements—all lying within the Nuclear Area of North China where the three modern provinces of Honan, Shansi and Shensi come together—belong to the neolithic stage of Chinese civilization called "Yang-shao", after a site in Shensi. In all of them were found the preserved seeds of millet, a grain conspicuously native to northern China.

A typical example of these settlements was Pan-p'o, which stood near a small tributary of the river Weishui around 4000 B.C. The village, which may have had as many as 600 inhabitants, covered more than seven acres and was surrounded by a ditch whose purpose was drainage, defence, or both. The dwellings, constructed of wattle-and-daub, with roofs supported by wooden pillars, were built partially underground (*pages 56-57*). Their low, tunnel-like entryways, like those of many Eskimo houses, faced south, presumably to avoid cold northerly winds and to help conserve warmth inside. In the centre of the village stood a large building covering 136 square yards that, judging from its size, may have served some communal purposes.

Pan-p'o was thus quite an advanced settlement. Moreover, its agriculture was sufficiently advanced to feed 600 people. Among its ruins, seeds of foxtail millet (*Setaria italica*) were found by the bushel in pits and other storage places. Traces of the same grain showed up at other agricultural sites in the neighbourhood. The villages of the area also yielded stone sickles, hoes and spades not very much different from those uncovered at An-yang—further proof that Yang-shao farming was already fairly sophisticated by 4000 B.C. If agriculture had reached this stage of development by then, the first domestication of millet probably had been accomplished many centuries before.

But just what earlier farming in China was like remains to some extent unknown. This is partly because the country's chaotic state during the first half of the 20th Century, a period marked by almost continuous warfare and anarchy, seriously hampered the work of archaeologists probing the ancient past. Nevertheless, some information about the beginnings of Chinese agriculture can be inferred by studying ancient Chinese literature. The *Book of Odes*, for example, written during the Chou Dynasty that followed the Shang rulers and lasted until about 200 B.C., makes it plain that millet was still the most important food crop in North China.

An occasional passage in the *Book of Odes* hints that another food source—cultivated wheat—may have arrived overland from western Asia in later years. A further hint that wheat was a late arrival comes from the Chinese written word for wheat itself. While the character for millet contains the root word *ho*, which means "cereal plant", the names for wheat and barley are derived from the character *lai*, which means "come", suggesting that wheat and barley had come to China from somewhere else.

Wheat must have been difficult to grow in the loess country, and the fact that it was grown at all is a tribute to the Chinese farmer. As late as the First Century B.C. a famous agricultural treatise, *Fan Sheng-chih shu*, describes the elaborate way in which it should be planted: "If at the time of wheat planting the weather has been rainless and dry for some time, first soak the wheat seeds in a thin starchy gruel which

Made in northern China around 4000 B.C., this elegant storage vessel for millet is only one of nearly a thousand pieces of fried pottery unearthed by Chinese archaeologists in the ruins of the farming village of Pan-p'o between 1954 and 1957. It consists of three parts: a tapered jar, a tight-fitting, dome-shaped lid and a cap—perhaps used as a bowl or scoop.

56

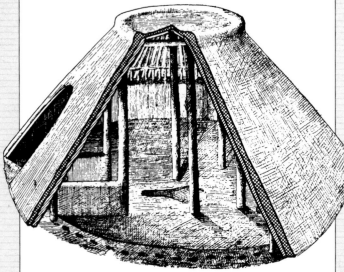

The round house above, reconstructed from on-site evidence (top), typifies 31 of the dwellings found in the 4000 B.C. village of Pan-p'o. This mud-and-grass structure was supported by six posts surrounding its central hearth. From the door at left, a dirt ramp descended to the dug-out floor, 17 feet in diameter.

should be mixed with the excreta of silkworms. The seeds should be soaked at midnight and must be sown shortly before dawn, so that the gruel and the ground dew will go down into the soil.''

This laborious procedure suggests that wheat was still poorly adapted to the North China climate. The soaking beforehand was obviously designed to give the seed a head start. In its Middle Eastern places of origin, wheat had been adapted to rather mild, rainy winters during which the plant developed its roots and leaves. Its grains formed and ripened in the hot, dry early summer.

In North China, by contrast, the cold winters are rather dry and what rain there is falls mostly in summer. Not until spring wheat—sown in spring for harvesting in autumn—arrived much later from the West did wheat become a crop that the farmers of North China could grow dependably.

Certainly more important than wheat, and perhaps nearly as important as millet, to the well-being of the ancient inhabitants of northern China were soya beans, which provided both the protein and oil essential for a rounded diet. In China soya beans eventually became the equivalent of the West's protein-rich milk and cheese, and they still are that today. The beans can be served in innumerable ways, some of which counterfeit meat and have almost the same nutritional value. There is even soya milk that can be fed to babies. (Interestingly, adult Chinese have difficulty digesting cow's milk, a fact that seems to have limited the importance of cattle in their country.)

Several wild varieties of soya beans are native to northern China, and to judge again from such ancient literary sources as the *Book of Odes*, the beans began to be cultivated there in Shang times, between

1600 and 1100 B.C. The archaeological evidence tends to bear this out. Soya beans have not been found in the villages of the early millet farmers, and the skeletons of the farmers themselves indicate that they were a small, weak-boned people, possibly suffering from a protein deficiency that soya beans might have helped to correct.

Once soya beans came under widespread cultivation, they added not only essential elements to the diet of the ancient Chinese but nutrients to the soil itself—thus helping to keep it fertile. Soya beans are legumes whose roots have nodules of symbiotic bacteria to capture gaseous atmospheric oxygen and make it available to the plant as a dissolved compound. When the roots rot, they contribute their nutrients to the soil. This fact is well known to modern farmers, who plant such legumes as alfalfa, clover and peas on land that was used the season before by such nitrogen-demanding crops as wheat and corn. Chinese farmers may have understood this benefit in very early times. In writings older than the *Book of Odes*, the character *shu*, for soya bean, shows at its bottom a row of short strokes some scholars think symbolize fertilizing nodules on the plant's roots.

Rice, the staple food of China today, evidently meant much less to the early Chinese than soya beans. Rice seems to have been first domesticated in the southern part of the country, thousands of miles from the region where millet and soya bean farming were born. A semitropical plant that prefers warm, moist conditions, it does not grow wild in the loess country; even today it can be grown there only with difficulty. But in the south, especially around the mouth of the river Yangtze where the climate is warm and the rainfall heavy, many kinds of rice still

Along with round houses (opposite page), Pan-p'o village had 15 rectangular dwellings. The remnants of this one (photograph) measure 18 feet by 18 feet. The square houses resembled the round ones in their construction, as the drawing indicates: the pitched roof was made of thatch and the floor was recessed. The entrance, in this case, was a covered passageway.

grow wild. From here—on a site near Shanghai—comes the earliest known, undeniably domesticated rice. It dates from around 3000 B.C. and is far enough removed from any wild ancestor to indicate that rice was already a well-established cereal crop in southern China by that time.

The farmers of the Middle East and northern China both got their start by learning how to cultivate annual grasses—wheat and millet—that propagate by seed. But in tropical Southeast Asia an entirely different kind of agriculture arose, based on the edible roots of such perennials as taro and yams. How early is uncertain. In this region, comprising modern Thailand, Burma, Indochina, eastern India and southernmost China, root crops still form an important part of the diet. If they were cultivated there in very ancient times, however, they failed to lift the prehistoric inhabitants closer to civilization than the semigathering level. Perhaps the reason is that tropical root culture is too easy—requiring, in the case of some plants, no more effort than is necessary to poke around the roots with a digging stick and break off pieces just below the ground. The plant does not die, but continues to grow and produce more roots—an ever-replenishing source of food. Other plants must be pried out of the soil to get at their roots, but even these, after part is removed, start growing again if stuck back in the ground. Many primitive tropical root growers follow this root-cutting practice today, as their ancestors did many thousands of years ago.

However lackadaisical the approach to cultivation may have been in Southeast Asia, several recent, but highly controversial, discoveries suggest a very respectable antiquity for agriculture in that part of the

Finding the Ancient Ancestor of Modern Corn

For years botanists puzzled over the origin of domesticated corn. No wild plant like it existed—yet surely it had a wild ancestor. Then, in the 1950s, came the answer. While probing the earth 227 feet under Mexico City, a team of geologists turned up 19 large grains of fossil pollen. Palynologists who examined the grains guessed they might have come from corn; but their date—estimated at 80,000 years ago—set them long before corn's domestication. Was the pollen from modern corn's wild ancestor? To find out, palynologists first compared it, under a standard microscope, with pollen of modern corn and of Tripsacum, a grass some supposed was domesticated corn's progenitor. The fossil pollen looked more like the modern pollen than that of Tripsacum. For confirmation, the scientists studied all three types under a scanning electron microscope. Enlarged some 900 times (*second column, right*), all three looked dissimilar. But magnified 6,000 times (*third column*), the ancient and modern corn pollens showed surfaces so alike—and so unlike Tripsacum's—that the researchers concluded they came from directly related plants, one the other's ancestor.

Pollen grains of Tripsacum grass (top row), ancient wild corn (middle row) and modern corn (bottom row) are compared in increasing magnifications. When enlarged about 900 times, the wild corn pollen (centre picture) looks collapsed and tattered; but magnified about 6,000 times, its regular, caviar-like surface bears a closer resemblance to the modern corn pollen than to the irregular lumpy surface of Tripsacum.

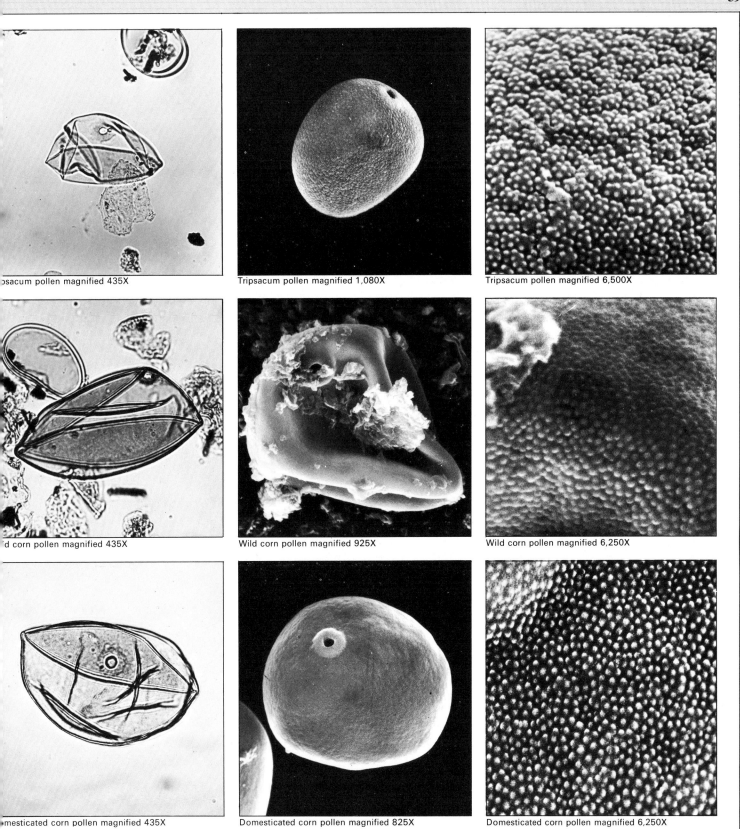

Tripsacum pollen magnified 435X

Tripsacum pollen magnified 1,080X

Tripsacum pollen magnified 6,500X

Wild corn pollen magnified 435X

Wild corn pollen magnified 925X

Wild corn pollen magnified 6,250X

Domesticated corn pollen magnified 435X

Domesticated corn pollen magnified 825X

Domesticated corn pollen magnified 6,250X

world. One intriguing find was made in 1966 by Chester F. Gorman, who was still a student at the University of Hawaii when he excavated Spirit Cave in northwestern Thailand. Among the debris left by the inhabitants of the cave, and dating between 10,000 and 6000 B.C., Gorman found the remains of plants that seemed to indicate that the people living there were cultivating two kinds of Old World broad beans and a variety of pea as early as 7000 B.C. —about a thousand years after the earliest plant domestication in the Middle East. Gorman also made another intriguing discovery, in the form of fragments of slate knives that were like the rice-reaping knives used today by Javanese farmers. This find suggested to Gorman that rice was a crop in Thailand some 500 years before it was cultivated in China.

At about the same time that Gorman was excavating Spirit Cave, a team of archaeologists from the University of Hawaii and the University of Otago in New Zealand dug into a low mound called Non Nok Tha in eastern Thailand. From the lower levels of the village that had stood there in 3500 B.C. the excavators recovered the remains of carbonized rice chaff. Since it was found in pottery fragments, it was presumed to be chaff from domesticated rice. If this interpretation is correct, it gives further support to those who believe that rice was being grown in Southeast Asia several centuries before it is known to have been grown in southern China.

While agriculture was springing up in Asia, it also began appearing in both Mexico and Peru. Which region developed it first is now a matter of archaeological debate, but its early stages can be most clearly traced in Mexico.

Of all the land north of the Isthmus of Panama, Mexico was the most likely place for farming to appear. Because of its mountain terrain, it provided many different growing conditions, ranging from dry to wet and from hot to cool. Consequently, it possessed an enormous variety of edible wild-plant species from which incipient Indian agriculturists could make their selection. One of these was corn (maize), the food that would ultimately play a major rôle in the rise of such splendid Indian civilizations as the Mayan and the Aztec.

But Mexico also had a great disadvantage; it lacked anything comparable to the rich stands of wild wheat and barley that encouraged Middle Eastern hunter-gatherers to settle down near these natural granaries and establish villages even before they invented agriculture. This may be one reason why settled life seems to have been a relatively late development in Mexico and neighbouring parts of Central America, with the result that no high Indian civilization appeared there until around 1000 B.C., long after civilizations had grown up in the Middle East.

Still, there is evidence to suggest that the beginnings of Mexican agriculture were much earlier. The oldest hints of cultivation discovered so far in this area come from some caves in the state of Tamaulipas on the Gulf of Mexico, just south of the Rio Grande. In the 1950s Richard S. MacNeish, an anthropologist then of the National Museum of Canada, excavated several of these caves. In them he uncovered human debris and plant remains that had been preserved for thousands of years by the dryness of the caves. In one cave, he found among the deepest deposits of human refuse six seeds of a kind of squash ancestral to pumpkins and summer squash.

The Rise of Farming in a Mexican Valley

One of the most thorough studies of man's transition from a hunter and gatherer to a settled farmer was carried out in the 1960s in Mexico's Tehuacán Valley. There an expedition excavated 12 sites, including caves, and collected some 100,000 plant specimens and 11,000 animal bones. The results are schematized in the charts below, which show the gradual changes in diet and food production of the valley's inhabitants over 7,000 years.

What the Tehuacán Indians Ate

As farming methods improved in the Tehuacán Valley, the Indian diet began to broaden from its original base of wild plants and animal foods around 6000 B.C. Squash and beans gradually gained in importance, but after 3000 B.C. corn became a major staple, supplementing and in part supplanting many other forms of food the Indians had relied on. Although domesticated dog and turkey and some wild animals were still eaten, corn had become the Indians' major source of nourishment by A.D. 1000.

How They Grew It

The most primitive type of farming practised at first was horticulture, the somewhat haphazard planting of seeds on small plots. Hydro-horticulture, which involved carrying water from streams to the plants, represented some improvement. But the major advance took place with fully-fledged agriculture—the systematic cultivation of plants on large plots. Finally, irrigation agriculture freed the Indians from dependence on a short rainy season and allowed them to raise not one but several crops a year.

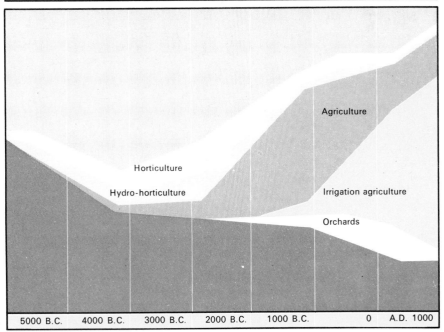

Wild plants

Cultivated squash and beans

Cultivated corn

Cultivated fruit and seed plants

Domesticated dog and turkey

Big and small game

Agriculture

Horticulture

Hydro-horticulture

Irrigation agriculture

Orchards

6000 B.C.   5000 B.C.   4000 B.C.   3000 B.C.   2000 B.C.   1000 B.C.   0   A.D. 1000

The three smaller seeds MacNeish believed to be wild, but because the other three were larger they appeared to have been cultivated. And when carbon-dated, these larger seeds proved to have come from squash that grew about 7000 B.C. This discovery would put the start of Mexican agriculture fairly close to the beginnings of farming in the Middle East.

Another Tamaulipas cave thoroughly investigated by MacNeish, and radiocarbon-dated by him between 5000 and 3000 B.C., yielded not only large squash seeds that were undoubtedly cultivated but also two varieties of cultivated beans, ancestors of the beans that are now staple crops in Mexico and many other parts of the world.

In domesticating these common beans, *Phaseolus vulgaris* and *P. lunatus*, the ancient farmers were assisted by the beans themselves. In the wild forms, which still grow in Mexico, the seeds are borne in pods that split apart when ripe, twisting into spirals and throwing the seeds violently in all directions. This provided an effective dispersal system for the beans, but impeded the harvesting of the pods; they had to be gathered before they exploded and scattered their seeds. Luckily the Mexican beans—like the easily shattered wild wheat of the Middle East—occasionally produced aberrant individuals whose pods did not explode when ripe. These were gathered in larger proportion by foraging Indians, and when they came to be planted they fathered nonexploding races of cultivated beans.

The most important crop of ancient Mexico is also the subject of a fascinating mystery. The crop is corn. And the key to the mystery is the ancestor of this staple of Mexican agriculture. Unlike any other food crop, corn has never been found growing in its wild state. Various tall, coarse grasses that look like corn grow in Mexico and farther south; some of these grasses even bear their seeds on the sides of their stalks, as corn does. But none of them is corn, and no attempts by ancient planters to breed these grasses could have made them into corn.

Furthermore, the earliest domesticated corn that has so far been found is remarkable botanically: it is of a type that cannot release its seeds without help from man. Its kernels, arranged in tight rows on the cob, are enclosed in tough husks. If the corn cobs are left unharvested in the field, they eventually fall to the ground and the seed-kernels go to waste; they cannot sprout unless the husk is opened by some outside agency, usually man. In short, the earliest corn that has been discovered had to be planted and cultivated. The Aztecs, who did cultivate corn, realized this, and assigned corn a divine origin. One of their oral traditions explains: "Once again the gods asked, 'Oh you gods, what is man to eat?' And a search was begun high and low for a food. It was then that the red ant brought back corn seed from the land of plenty (the underworld)."

Because of this dependence of corn on man, some botanists theorized that corn did not actually originate in the Americas after all, but was brought to the New World from somewhere else, perhaps Asia, where wild corn might still be growing. Botanists have never found any wild corn in Asia, and the theory in fact lasted only until 1954, when a drill sunk 200 feet below Mexico City brought up an earth sample containing 19 grains of fossil corn pollen (*page 59*). Geologists proved that the soil—and accordingly the pollen—was more than 80,000 years old. Since man had not reached the New World at that early

Text continued on page 67

Sacrificial Rites for the Gods of Agriculture

The Aztecs worshipped a multitude of agricultural gods whose favours, they believed, could be bestowed and retracted with equal ease and whose spirits therefore needed to be placated if crops were to succeed. According to Aztec mythology, many earlier gods had sacrificed themselves to bring life and food to man in ancient times, and those who remained, or had been born since, were always hungry. Sometimes these gods could be appeased by peaceful ceremonies; but the best way to placate them was by human sacrifice, which satisfied the gods' sanguinary appetites. Most rites thus had a fair share of gore (*overleaf*).

Though there were numerous deities, two figured importantly in agricultural rituals. One was Tlaloc, the rain god; the other was Chicomecoatl, the corn goddess. Ceremonies pertaining to each are shown on the following pages in illustrations that, like the one at right, were painted by the Indians.

A Spirited Summer Festival

In a ceremony called the falling of fruits, men with blackened bodies link hands to execute a sacred dance around a decorated tree. In the foreground, a paper-crowned priest beats on a drum, while another on a platform directs the movement. After the dance, men scrambled up the tree, which had been shorn of branches and bark to make it slippery. The first to grasp the packages of food on the trunk and hurl them to people below was honoured by the priests.

64

The Corn Goddess' Bloody Week
In September the Aztecs held a week-long harvest rite for Chicomecoatl, the corn goddess, in which a young woman, dressed as the goddess, was sacrificed. Her head was cut off and her body was flayed, whereupon a priest put on her skin to impersonate Chicomecoatl (right). Holding the goddess' symbol, corn, he was led in procession to a temple, where he was dressed in an elaborate costume (below). At week's end he took off the skin, and it was laid, with the woman's head, on an ornate bed (far right).

With his hands thrust through the sacrificed woman's skin and the victim's hands dangling from his wrists, the priest carries ears of corn.

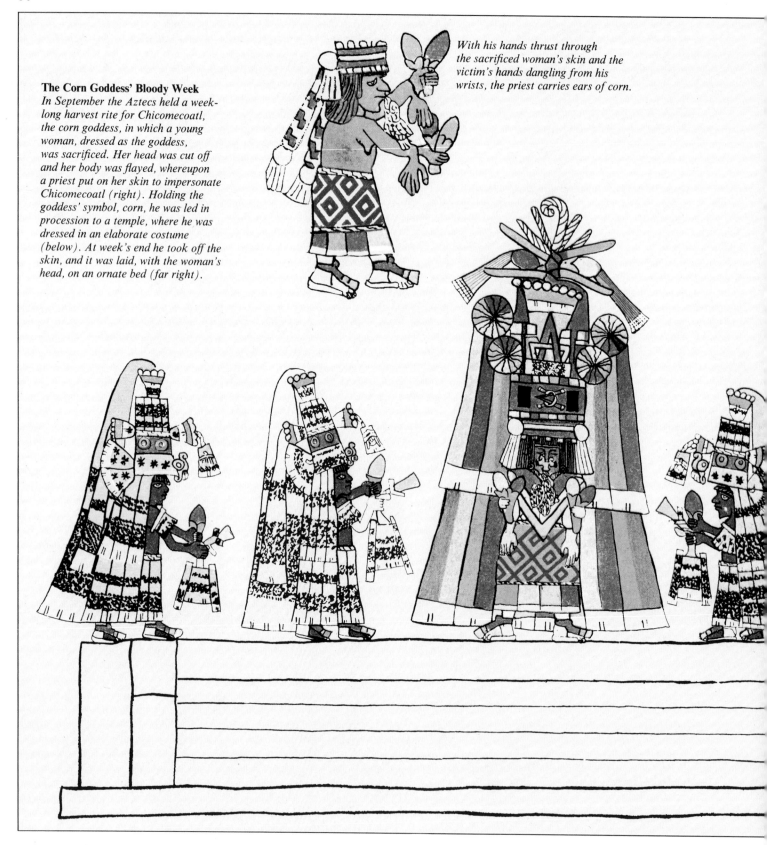

Attendants reassemble the victim's head and skin, which they deck out on a bed.

Richly attired as Chicomecoatl, the priest is flanked by representatives of Tlaloc, the rain god, without whose ministrations there would be no crops.

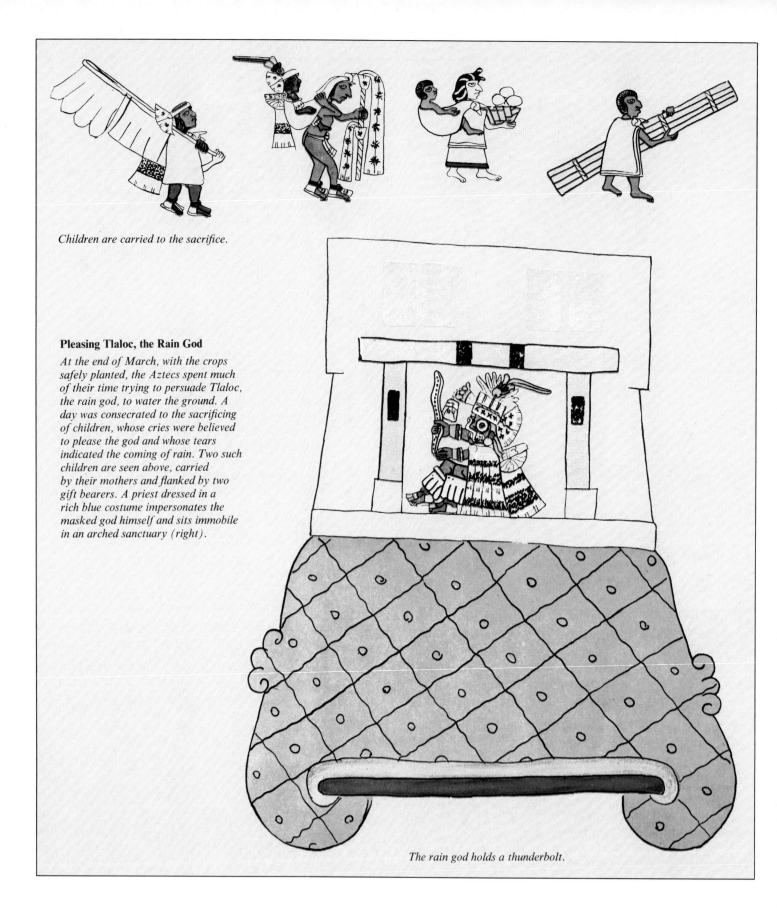

Children are carried to the sacrifice.

Pleasing Tlaloc, the Rain God

At the end of March, with the crops safely planted, the Aztecs spent much of their time trying to persuade Tlaloc, the rain god, to water the ground. A day was consecrated to the sacrificing of children, whose cries were believed to please the god and whose tears indicated the coming of rain. Two such children are seen above, carried by their mothers and flanked by two gift bearers. A priest dressed in a rich blue costume impersonates the masked god himself and sits immobile in an arched sanctuary (right).

The rain god holds a thunderbolt.

stage, the only possible conclusion that could be drawn was that this must have been the pollen of a wild native corn.

Encouraged by this evidence, MacNeish and his associates continued their search for further proof, particularly in the Tehuacán Valley in southern Mexico. The valley is now extensively irrigated and supports a large population, but in its natural state it was arid, and its vegetation consisted mostly of drought-resistant plants such as cacti, maguey and mesquite. Ranged at various levels in rocky outcrops around its bottom are caves where vegetable matter hardly decays at all.

To judge from the most ancient traces of human life found in the caves, the valley in its natural state supported a few "microbands" of hunter-gatherers who survived on deer, rabbits and such poor desert fare as cactus fruits, mesquite pods and the tough roots of maguey (*page 61*). They also gathered the seeds of a tall grass that grew in comparatively well-watered places like the alluvial fans of streams debouching on the valley floor. Finally, in one cave, in soil dating between 5200 and 3400 B.C., MacNeish found some tiny corn cobs. They were only about one inch long. Their kernels were gone—no doubt eaten by the people who had picked the ears so long ago. But each cob appeared to have been enclosed in a husk that opened when the kernels ripened. Moreover the kernels seemed to have been attached loosely to the cob, and thus could have dropped off or been blown off by the wind.

But what happened to this likely wild ancestor of corn? The answer depends upon a fundamental difference between corn and wheat. Both are annual grasses, but wheat is almost always self-pollinated. Each individual wheat flower is enclosed in such a way that pollen from outside rarely reaches it; the female parts are therefore fertilized by pollen from the male parts of the same flower. This withdrawn behaviour makes wheat resistant to hybridization. Crosses with closely related grasses are possible and seem to have happened on rare occasions, but they have had comparatively little effect. After 9,000 years of cultivation, wheat has improved as a crop but still looks very much like wild wheat.

Corn is at the other extreme of plant behaviour; it is exuberantly cross-pollinated. The male flowers are in the tassel at the tip of the stalk; they produce great quantities of pollen, which is carried long distances by the wind. The female flowers appear on the same plant, but their receptive parts are the silks that protrude from the young ears growing part way down the stalks. They are open to fertilization by any suitable pollen that hits them, whether it comes from their own plant, another corn plant or from a closely related grass. So hybridization is common—not an extreme rarity, as in wheat.

This explains why, around 1500 B.C., corn changed radically and suddenly became the leading crop of the Tehuacán Valley and other parts of Mexico. Botanical evidence indicates that the improved variety was the result of hybridization between the wild-type corn and a near relative, a grass called *teosinte*. There is nothing unlikely about this. Such crosses still appear in Mexico where *teosinte* grows wild near fields of cultivated corn. The effect of the early but productive crosses was dramatic. With the new, more productive corn, population increased; large villages appeared; the cultural level rose towards what can be described as incipient civilization.

Plants grown by Peruvian Indians as early as 4000 B.C. are portrayed by the makers of these ceramic jars. The peanut (below) and the potato (right) have human faces representing the plants' spirits. The third jar shows a squash with a monkey on top, the spout projecting from the monkey's back.

So what happened to wild corn apparently was this: it was a victim of its sexual permissiveness. It was probably never very common, growing only in a few habitats such as slopes that received extra water from flooded streams. In these favoured places the early farmers planted their improved hybrid corn, whose husks kept the seeds from dispersing naturally. Clouds of pollen rose from the cultivated fields, were carried far by the wind and sought out the wild corn plants. When it fertilized their female flowers, the result was death; the ravaged plants produced ears wrapped so tightly in husks that the seeds could not disperse and grow. This continued for thousands of years. Eventually wild corn was swamped with death-dealing pollen and became extinct.

Mexico and Peru are only 1,500 miles apart, and in most parts of the world such close neighbours would have been profoundly influenced by each other's developments. But the tangled jungles and rough terrain of the Isthmus of Panama and neighbouring parts of Colombia present a formidable barrier. They are roadless even now, almost trailless, and inhabited only by a few Indians

It is unlikely that any knowledge of farming penetrated this barrier from Mexico to Peru—or the other way around—at a very early date. Peruvian crops either differed from those of Mexico or seem to have been developed independently from wild plants that were common to both areas. Later contacts between the Mexican and South American farmers appear to have been nil. When the Spanish conquerors arrived in the early 16th Century, neither the Aztecs of Mexico nor the Incas of Peru had any knowledge of each other's existence.

Because of Peru's peculiar geography, its early farmers had to contend with more extreme conditions than did the Mexicans. Most of the country is occupied by the tall, steep ranges of the Andes, which rise so high that the fertile valleys tucked between them are cool, some of them chilly all the year round, even though they lie only a few degrees of latitude from the equator. These well-watered, grassy uplands were full of game and therefore attractive to hunters, who may have populated them sparsely as long ago as 15,000 B.C.

On the Pacific side of the Andes, on the seacoast, the land is strikingly different. An ocean current flowing up from Antarctica and along the coast cools the prevailing winds blowing from the west and wrings most of the moisture out of them. Damp, cold fogs are common, but only in one year out of about 25 does rain fall in any measurable quantity. Not surprisingly, most of the Peruvian coast is an absolute desert, as bare of life as a new-laid gravel road. Only where swift rivers flow down from the Andes do patches of green appear, each a verdant oasis.

The ancient inhabitants of these fertile spots developed a sophisticated civilization. Many curious and beautiful things—among them delicate, richly patterned textiles, finely modelled and painted pottery and intricate ornaments wrought in gold and silver—have come out of graves in coastal Peru where these elaborate cultures arose.

But it was a fairly late development. Apparently the extensive agriculture that led to this civilization did not develop in this peculiar habitat before 2500 B.C. One reason may have been that a few squashes and gourds were the only wild plants in these areas suitable for domestication. Another reason could be

Around the Year with Inca Farmers

August. *In a symbolic ceremony, the Inca emperor and noblemen turn over the first earth in a sacred field, while three women bow and the empress offers corn beer.*

September. *With an ornate digging stick, a farmer punches holes into which a woman scatters corn seeds. The Incas believed women planters ensured successful crops.*

October. *Wearing a wolfskin to look more formidable, and carrying a sling and a noisemaker, a boy tries to scare birds and a skunk from the sprouting fields.*

February. *To keep hungry foxes, deer and birds from eating up the swelling ears of corn, a woman creates a frightening din by beating incessantly on her drum.*

March. *As the harvest ripens, birds attack the corn with renewed appetite, but the young boy, with his sling and stick, is once again on hand to scare them away.*

April. *A thief skulking along the rows of ripened corn can do even more damage than a hungry llama; the farmer at watch before the fire remains oblivious of his presence.*

The drawings below depict the seasonal working of Inca farmlands, starting with the month of August—the lower hemisphere's late-winter planting time. The artist, a Peruvian of Indian-Spanish blood who sent the drawings in the 1580s to the King of Spain as part of a treatise on Inca life, labelled them with an odd mixture of Spanish and Quechuan words.

November. *A woman irrigates fields with water from a small reservoir. The Incas depended on irrigation in this month of little rain when the rivers often dried up.*

December. *To plant potatoes, one woman inserts the tubers into a hole in the earth made by the man, while another stands by to smooth the soil with a cultivating tool.*

January. *Wielding primitive hoes, a couple cultivates its fields in the rain. Another farmer sits before a fire and keeps a sharp eye out for crop robbers.*

May. *Harvest time brings a division of labour. While a man cuts stalks, his female helper carries bundles of them on her back to the field where she lets them dry.*

June. *With the aid of a digging stick and a hoe, a man and woman root potatoes from the ground. Another woman transports them in heavy sacks to a storage place.*

July. *At the end of the harvest, potatoes are brought by llama to a state warehouse and placed there. The emperor could distribute surplus food in time of need.*

that the coastal people felt no pressing need to till the soil; the quantities of fishbones and shells found in the remains of their settlements show how effectively they had learned to harvest the sea, which in that part of the world was extremely rich. When they finally did resort to extensive agriculture, it was not an invention of their own. Crops seem to have arrived on the coast fully domesticated, presumably from the Andean valleys.

Up in the valleys, in contrast to the coastal regions, agriculture was well developed. But when archaeologists try to trace its development, they run into sizeable difficulties. Andean Peru, with its rugged mountains and steep valleys, is a hard country to travel in, let alone to work in. Moreover, its comparatively humid climate does not ordinarily favour the preservation of plant remains. The hot, jungle-covered lands on the eastern slopes of the Andes, where some of the crops may have originated, present even greater physical obstacles to archaeologists searching for plant origins.

But investigation of agriculture in Andean Peru is an eminently worthwhile undertaking, for farming here provided the base on which the predecessors of the Incas and the Incas themselves built their extraordinary civilizations. The mountain farmers were the first to grow white and sweet potatoes, tomatoes, peanuts and lima beans. That they were excellent farmers is attested to by some of the pottery found in pre-Inca graves. Using living vegetables as their models, Peruvian potters created vessels that copy faithfully the shape and texture of potatoes, squashes, chillies and other plant foods (*page 68*). These ancient vegetables reproduced in clay look so healthy and so well developed that any modern housewife would be glad to add them to her shopping bag.

The most important food raised in the mountains was the potato. Over 90 wild potato species are still found growing in the highlands, and literally hundreds of cultivated varieties, many of them developed by prehistoric farmers, are raised there by the Indians today and form a good part of their diet. Some of these are recognizable in present-day Indian markets as the common white potato, but others come in a remarkable assortment of colours, including pinkish-grey, purple and black, and there are even streaked or spotted potatoes.

All these were eaten by the ancient Peruvians, who learned how to preserve them in case of famine. Since potatoes are moist and therefore perishable, the Indians devised a way of converting them into a dried food that could be stored almost indefinitely. In a process that has come down to modern highland Indians, potatoes were placed in the cold mountain air where they were allowed alternately to freeze and thaw. Off and on over four or five days the Indians trampled them with their feet to squeeze out the moisture. The final product, known as *chuno* by today's Indians, was a fully dehydrated potato that could be stored whole or ground up into potato flour.

Besides potatoes, many other root crops with exotic local names such as *oca, ulluca* and *anu* have also been cultivated in the highlands since ancient times. So has *quinoa*, the only grain crop that does well at the highest altitudes; its small white, red or black seeds, used by the present-day Indians in soups, split when boiled and send out white threads that look like fine noodles.

The early farmers of the Andes may also have cultivated common beans as early as—and perhaps even earlier than—the Mexicans. While digging in the debris on the floor of a cave in the northern highlands, a team of archaeologists and botanists led by Lawrence Kaplan of the University of Massachusetts recently turned up 30 well-preserved beans dating to around 5600 B.C. Their comparatively large size showed that they had been cultivated (the wild beans of both Mexico and South America are always small). Further evidence of domestication came from two fragments of pod found with the beans. Both lacked the inner fibrous layer that makes the pods of wild beans twist open when they are ripe, scattering the seeds widely.

But what about corn, that staple of the American diet which is believed to have originated in Mexico and been transported to Peru? In 1970 an expedition, under the same Richard S. MacNeish who had discovered the earliest known traces of Mexican corn in the caves of Tehuacán Valley, went to Peru with a group of scientists and excavated a cave close to Ayacucho in the central Peruvian Andes. Much to everyone's amazement they found primitive corn cobs buried here that apparently date between 4300 and 2800 B.C., well before corn had become a major crop in Mexico. And the cobs did not resemble those of primitive Mexican corn.

So it is quite possible that the final clue to the mystery of corn's origins was uncovered in that cave high in the Peruvian Andes. Corn may have been first domesticated in Peru. It may eventually have been taken north, where it imparted to Mexican corn some of the new vigour that the crop started to show there around A.D. 700. It was about the same time that the improved, high-yielding Mexican corn is known to have begun slowly expanding northwards and eastwards across what is now the United States, reaching the Indians of New England about A.D. 1400. It is thus possible that the type of corn that was so important to the first European colonists may have had ancestors as far away as Peru.

Chapter Four: The Essential Addition—Livestock

Ganj-Dareh, a small mound in the mountains of western Iran, marks the site of an early neolithic settlement that flourished around 7000 B.C. In 1969 archaeologists from the University of Montreal, probing amidst its remains, discovered walls built of sun-baked mud bricks. This in itself was not a particularly surprising find; older mud-brick walls had turned up in the Middle East. What did startle and delight the excavators were several bricks that bore the unmistakable hoofprints of goats or sheep. Bones of both goats and sheep were known from earlier Middle East village sites, but whether they represented wild or protected animals was debatable.

At Ganj-Dareh there was no such doubt—the hoofprints were unquestionably those of domesticated animals. The reason the archaeologists knew this is that the animals that left the prints in the drying clay must have roamed the village more or less at will, as livestock often do in present-day Iranian villages. It is hard to imagine that wild goats or sheep would have been bold enough to invade Ganj-Dareh with its human inhabitants.

This is not to suggest that the domestication of animals originated with the villagers of Ganj-Dareh. Where or when man and his barnyard friends first formed their partnership can never be traced with exactness. But most of the evidence so far indicates that it began somewhere in the Middle East around 8000 B.C., with the rise of permanent settlements. Like

A ritual vessel in the shape of a pig, made of fired clay about 5600 B.C. in the Turkish village of Hacilar, suggests that the pig may have been among the livestock kept by the inhabitants. Pigs like this one, bearing tusks that modern farmers usually clip, are known to have been domesticated in the Middle East by 7000 B.C., some 1,500 years after sheep.

communal life and plant cultivation, it could not have happened suddenly in one particular village but instead developed gradually over a period of thousands of years. And the domestication included not only food-producing animals but also beasts of burden and even household pets.

Before men settled down and learned to support themselves by raising crops, they lived in a world of wild animals. They ate them and occasionally were eaten by them. Since hunting was an important part of their livelihood, they had to know the animals' habits intimately so as to predict what their quarry would do at any particular moment. Even when not busy tracking them, the hunters must have been deeply preoccupied with the creatures around them, forever observing them, commenting on them and thinking about them.

This long-standing relationship between men and beasts was bound to have consequences. One was that men, with their superior intelligence, learned how to control the movements of animals. There is good reason to believe that even as far back as 30,000 to 40,000 years ago, when much of the northern hemisphere was covered with glaciers, mammoth hunters knew how to drive a small group of these great beasts into traps or to a convenient slaughtering ground, thereby saving the considerable effort of carrying home their meat. Driving mammoths to the slaughter would not have entitled ice-age men to call themselves mammoth herders, but it would distinguish them from hunters who merely stalked and killed their prey wherever they found it.

The people who lived in the Middle East about 12,000 years ago, soon after the glaciers to the north

Where Animals Were First Domesticated

Between 8500 B.C., when farmers of the Middle East first learned to tend sheep, and 1000 B.C., the earliest date that can be given for the husbanding of reindeer, at least 22 species of animals are known to have been domesticated from their wild counterparts. In that time creatures ranging from the shaggy yak of Tibet to the silk-producing moth of China, from the prolific guinea pig of Peru to the durable camel of Arabia were made useful partners of man. The maps on these two pages indicate the general areas of the world in which these animals were found, and the areas where they were first domesticated.

To determine such places and dates, the archaeologists must combine solid evidence with a more circumstantial kind. The bones of sheep, goats, pigs and cattle—which turn up throughout Europe and Asia—provide the most positive clues (*pages 81-84*). But when no bones exist or identification is uncertain, the scholars turn to secondary sources: the depiction of what look like domesticated chickens on 4,000-year-old figurines from Pakistan, for example; or a picture of a bee serving as the emblem of an Egyptian king who reigned around 3000 B.C. The researchers continue to dig, figuratively and literally, for the more tangible proof of their educated guesswork. And as a result, even more early domesticates will undoubtedly be added to the already impressive tally.

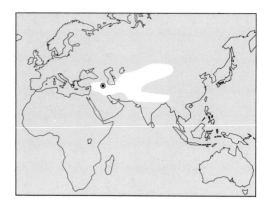

Wild Sheep: Western Asia
The map at left shows the range of wild sheep—an area comprising much of southwestern Asia. The earliest evidence of domestication was found at Zawi Chemi Shanidar in Iraq (dot).

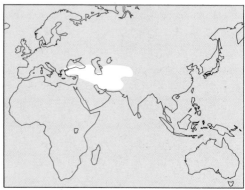

Wild Goats: Turkey to Afghanistan
The goat, the second animal to be domesticated by man, roamed wild from Turkey to eastern Afghanistan. Ganj-Dareh (dot), in Iran, yielded the earliest sign of goat domestication.

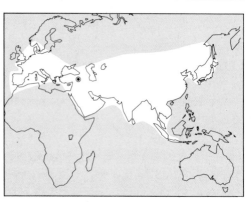

Wild Pigs: Europe and Asia
The ancestor of the domesticated pig was native to most of Europe and the southern half of Asia. The oldest known sign of its domestication was found at Çayönü in Turkey (dot).

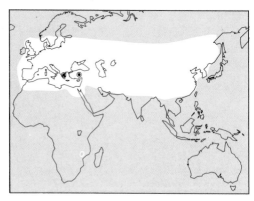

Wild Cattle: Europe, Africa, Asia
The aurochs, origin of domesticated cattle, was native to an expanse of Europe, North Africa and Asia. The oldest signs of its domestication come from Greece and Turkey (dots).

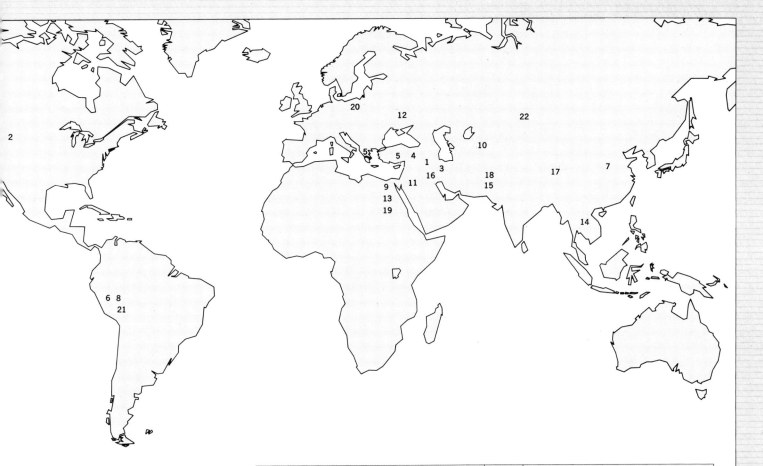

Global Range of First Domesticates
The map above shows sites where the oldest known evidence of animal domestication has been found. In the list at right, with symbols for the animals keyed by numbers to locations on the map, the sites' modern names are used with the approximate dates in chronological order that archaeologists have given to the finds.

1. **SHEEP** (8500 B.C.) Zawi Chemi Shanidar, Iraq	12. **HORSE** (3000 B.C.) Ukraine, U.S.S.R.
2. **DOG** (8400 B.C.) Jaguar Cave, Idaho	13. **HONEY BEE** (3000 B.C.) Nile Valley, Egypt
3. **GOAT** (7500 B.C.) Ganj-Dareh, Iran	14. **BANTENG** (3000 B.C.) Non Nok Tha, Thailand
4. **PIG** (7000 B.C.) Cayönü, Turkey	15. **WATER BUFFALO** (2500 B.C.) Indus Valley, Pakistan
5. **CATTLE** (6500 B.C.) Thessaly, Greece; Anatolia, Turkey	16. **DUCK** (2500 B.C.) Middle East
6. **GUINEA PIG** (6000 B.C.) Ayacucho Basin, Peru	17. **YAK** (2500 B.C.) Tibet
7. **SILK MOTH** (3500 B.C.) Hsi-yin-t'sun, China	18. **DOMESTIC FOWL** (2000 B.C.) Indus Valley, Pakistan
8. **LLAMA** (3500 B.C.) Andean Highlands, Peru	19. **CAT** (1600 B.C.) Nile Valley, Egypt
9. **ASS** (3000 B.C.) Nile Valley, Egypt	20. **GOOSE** (1500 B.C.) Germany
10. **BACTRIAN CAMEL** (3000 B.C.) Southern U.S.S.R.	21. **ALPACA** (1500 B.C.) Andean Highlands, Peru
11. **DROMEDARY** (3000 B.C.) Saudi Arabia	22. **REINDEER** (1000 B.C.) Pazyryk Valley, Siberia, U.S.S.R.

receded, were still nomadic hunter-gatherers. There were no mammoths around then (men had perhaps played an important part in their extinction), but the hills teemed with wild sheep and goats. These were very good to eat and reproduced so fast that many could be killed without actually curtailing the population. Like the ice-age mammoth hunters, the early goat and sheep hunters probably knew how to control the movements of their prey, at least to the extent of driving considerable numbers of the animals into pens or steep-walled ravines where they could be more easily killed.

Perhaps it was only inevitable that from the ubiquitous wild goats and sheep living in the hills of the Middle East should have sprung the world's first domesticated, food-producing animals—but just how this momentous development took place is largely a matter of conjecture. A long-favoured theory held that their domestication may have originally began with pet-keeping among the nomadic hunters. According to this engaging idea, fathers sometimes brought back from the hunt lambs or kids to entertain their wives and children. There is no evidence, however, that early hunters kept pets; even if they did, the pets probably did not survive long enough in a nomadic camp to breed. One tender-hearted authority seriously suggests that they may have been set free when the hunters packed up camp and moved on; it seems more likely that they were eaten.

In any case, by the beginning of neolithic times some 11,000 years ago, when the Middle Easterners started to settle in permanent (although not yet agricultural) communities, they began to keep goats and sheep—and not as occasional pets but in permanent flocks, to use as a food reserve. The evidence for this consists of bones from both kinds of animals found in refuse heaps. But when it comes to evaluating relics as ancient as these and differentiating between wild and domesticated animals, the experts confront a jungle of uncertainty.

For one thing, goats and sheep evolved from a distant but common ancestor, and their bones, in the earliest stages of domestication, look so much alike that it is hard to tell, especially from fragmentary remains, which belonged to goats and which to sheep. Even when the bones can be distinguished, determining whether they represent wild or domesticated sheep and goats is another problem. The natural thing to do, seemingly, would be to compare them with skeletons of wild sheep and goats that still roam remote and rugged parts of the Middle East. Domesticated goats are believed to have descended from the stockier, heavier bezoar (*Capra aegagrus*), and sheep from the Asiatic mouflon (*Ovis orientalis*), a sheeplike animal with scant wool. But these still-existing species may themselves be partly a creation of man. Some authorities think it possible, even probable, that shortly after domestication got underway, goats and sheep whose skeletal structure was already beginning to be modified by human intervention may have escaped and bred with the original wild species. Thus they would have passed some of their man-influenced traits to their wild relatives, making the bones virtually indistinguishable.

Despite such problems, archaeologists can still make some educated guesses about the bones they find. For instance, when they unearth a collection in which the remains of very old and very young individuals predominate, they speculate that the animals were wild, since both types would have been easiest for

primitive hunters to kill. On the other hand, if the bones include a disproportionately large number from good-sized but immature individuals, there is a fair chance that the animals were on the way to being domesticated, if they had not already been. These may have been slaughtered before they reached full maturity because they were already as big as they ever would be—and little would have been gained by feeding or caring for them any longer.

Such evidence does not always mean that the animals were domesticated. In the opinion of some authorities, it may indicate that the hunters of pre-agricultural Middle East villages were using a form of selective killing in order to conserve game. They surely must have noticed that sheep and goats are enthusiastically polygamous and that a single male could service many females. Acting on such knowledge, they may have killed and brought home only males, sparing females for breeding as modern deer hunters are often required to do by law.

Another step the hunters may have taken to protect their game was to kill off predators. Here was a task that must have appealed to early neolithic hunters. It demanded courage and skill, and the slain animals would have yielded trophies—a lion's mane, a leopard's skin, a wolf's fangs—to be shown at dances and ceremonials.

Precisely when the villagers began to keep food-producing animals in captivity is unknown. But whenever they took this step, it was a crucial one, for it marked the start of true domestication. Two aspects of the sheep's and goats' own behaviour worked in the villagers' favour. For one thing, both sheep and goats stick together in groups with recognized leaders. Moreover, a newborn lamb or kid shows great attachment for its mother, but if taken away from her at birth it will trustingly attach itself to a human protector. This easy transfer of allegiance, called "imprinting", occurs most strongly among mammals with herding instincts.

So, in a sense, the animals helped to domesticate themselves. Without this combination of traits—imprinting and a strong herding instinct—it probably would have been impossible for the Middle Easterners to build up flocks. The first step in that direction may have been to capture newborn wild lambs or kids whose mothers had been killed by hunters and carry them bleating back to the village. Feeding them would be a problem. They would be too young for their digestions to cope with grass, but perhaps human wet nurses could be persuaded to suckle them until they were old enough to graze (in primitive New Guinea villages today, women frequently breast feed piglets). Although a good many infant sheep and goats treated this way must have perished, others must have survived to reach maturity and breed. When their own offspring were born, feeding the young was no longer a problem. The mothers could suckle them, as well as any additional lambs or kids brought in from the wild. Thus a flock would grow rapidly, and the villagers would be in business as breeders of truly domesticated animals.

All this would not have been as easy as it sounds. Until agriculture was fairly well established, other food sources may have run low at times—and the animals may have been eaten. Or during the mating season, tame females might break for liberty to follow a magnificent wild male that had strutted down from the hills. And yet by about 7000 B.C. most Middle East villages seem to have acquired flocks of domesticated sheep or goats, or both.

Not long after these animals first came under man's care and protection, they began to undergo strange changes in anatomy. Natural selection in the wild guards against any departure from nature's established norm and penalizes it heavily if it is not to the species' advantage. Small males, for example, usually lose their battles for females and thus do not pass on genes that might perpetuate their slight build.

But when animals are taken under man's protection, his conscious or unconscious selection begins to modify them to fit his purpose. If a farmer wants a breed of small, docile sheep, he will begin to give small, docile rams all the ewes they can handle and slaughter the big, belligerent rams for food. Over the course of several generations the breed will become smaller, quieter and more tractable.

As such modifications began to occur in goats and sheep, the animals left in their skeletal remains evidence of these changes that scientists could interpret with assurance. In the case of both sheep and goats, the horns became conspicuously modified, and the bony cores that remained when the outer sheathing, a protein material called keratin, rotted away clearly showed the effects of domestication.

The ancient wild goats of the Middle East had smoothly curved, scimitar-shaped horns that were thicker on the outside (front of the curve) than on the inside. In cross section the horn cores are more or less four-sided, with one corner, that of the thin inside edge, sharper than the other three. The horns of wild sheep curve towards a circle and are almost flat in front. Cross sections of their cores are roughly oval, with the more pointed edge to the rear.

In the case of domesticated goats and sheep, the horns were modified in conspicuous ways. The horn cores of goats gradually lost their quadrilateral cross sections and became more oval. Later they started to twist into the corkscrew shape seen in the horns of many domesticated breeds in the Middle East today. The horn cores of sheep, on the other hand, became less flattened in front and in some domesticated breeds they developed a frontal ridge like that of wild goats. Female domesticated sheep even showed a tendency to lose their horns entirely.

Why such radical changes happened is something of a zoological mystery. It is unlikely that prehistoric breeders wanted to change horn shapes. More likely the changes were linked genetically to some other quality that the breeders wanted instead, such as a high milk yield in the case of goats, or woolliness in sheep. Whatever the case, the changes were transmitted to the offspring as the domesticated animals diverged more and more from their wild ancestors.

Text continued on page 85

Reading the Hidden Messages of the Bones

For generations archaeologists habitually threw away animal bones dug up in ancient dwelling sites, in the mistaken notion that only human remains and artifacts offer clues to man's history. In recent years, though, they have been saving these relics for laboratory study in the belief that such leftovers from prehistoric men's dinners might provide clues to the puzzle of when and where animals were first domesticated. Osteorchaeology—the study of ancient times through bones—is now a fully-fledged science, and it has developed highly sophisticated techniques for determining whether bone specimens belonged to wild animals or tame ones. Three methods are described on these pages.

The evidence presented by ancient goats' horns is perhaps the easiest for scientists to interpret. Depending on how far advanced in the domestication process the goats were, their horns show distinctly different characteristics—especially when they are examined in cross section (*right*). But a mystery that still remains to be resolved by other scientists is why the horns underwent such changes.

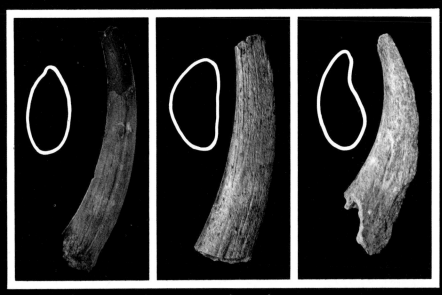

The cores of three goat horns from Iran trace changes that accompany domestication. The horn of a semidomesticated goat (left) is almond-shaped in cross section (white outline); that of a goat descended from many generations of domesticates is flat on one side (centre); an even longer period of domestication produces a kidney-shaped horn.

The hollow, bony core of a goat horn, unearthed at Iran's Ali Kosh and dating around 6500 B.C., bears the telltale mark of semidomestication: one side is flat, the other side forms a perfect crescent.

Clues Revealed in Polarized Light

Horns are not the only clues for the osteoarchaeologist. He can use other bones to distinguish prehistoric wild from tame animals. In some cases just size alone reveals a great deal (*page 84*). But other bone studies call for ingenious uses of complex equipment. One technique, adapted from a geological method of analysing rocks, uses polarized light to study the internal composition of bones. The specimen that lends itself best to this method is the humerus (uppermost part of forelimb) of either a sheep or a goat (*below*), sliced with a saw similar to a jeweller's stonecutter into thin slivers. The polarized light picks out minute features in the make-up of bone and thereby reveals interior structural differences that make it possible to distinguish between the bones of wild animals and those of animals that were tended by men.

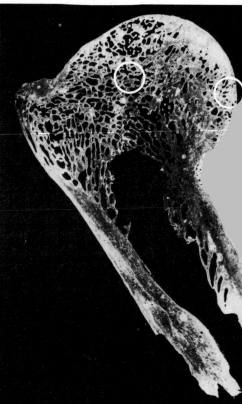

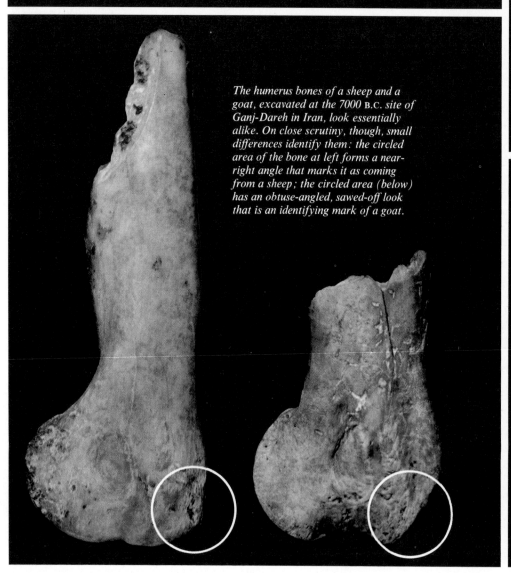

The humerus bones of a sheep and a goat, excavated at the 7000 B.C. site of Ganj-Dareh in Iran, look essentially alike. On close scrutiny, though, small differences identify them: the circled area of the bone at left forms a near-right angle that marks it as coming from a sheep; the circled area (below) has an obtuse-angled, sawed-off look that is an identifying mark of a goat.

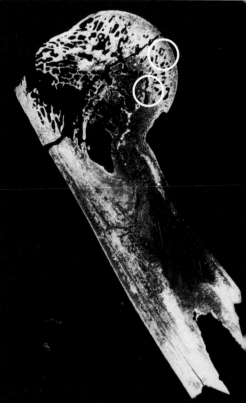

The interior structure of a wild sheep's humerus is shown in an unmagnified section at left (inner circle). Magnified 30 times (below) it displays the small holes with thick separating walls that give the bone a solidity that is needed for the activity of living in the wild.

The edge of the same wild sheep's humerus is uniform with the rest of the bone. This confirms that the animal was wild, because the polarized light, in exposing the mineral crystals of the bone, would pick up any changes caused by domestication (below).

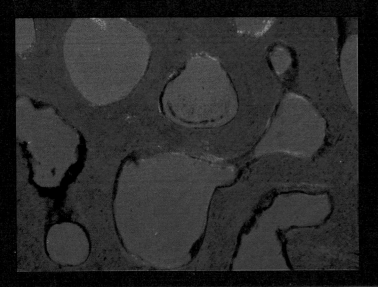

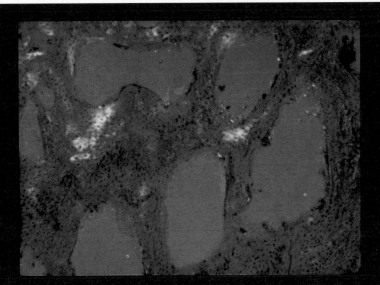
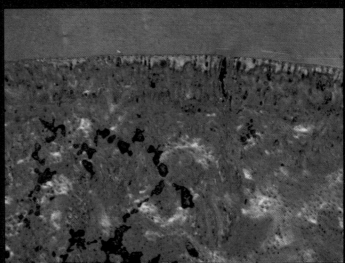

The inner portion (lower circle at left) of a tame sheep's humerus appears under the microscope (above) to be made up of long holes with rather thin walls between them, suggesting that domestication encouraged a less solid bone structure than in a wild animal.

The edge of the domesticated sheep's humerus (top circle on bone section at left) glows blue as the polarized light picks out the bone's mineral crystals that have aligned themselves to compensate for the internal weakness that is a result of domestication.

The Importance of Size

Often an ancient wild animal bone can be told from a domesticated one simply by comparing their sizes. Domesticated animals, unless deliberately bred large, tend to be smaller than their counterparts in the wild. Thus a seemingly trivial find such as a bovine foot bone can reveal a great deal when compared with a corresponding bone (*right*); and sometimes an important discovery can be made just by matching a few pigs' teeth (*below*).

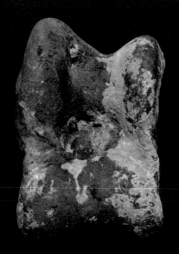 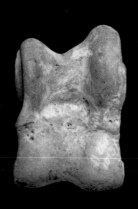

The hind-foot bones—called astragali—of two Middle Eastern cattle show a marked contrast in size. The left one, dated at about 6500 B.C., belonged to an aurochs, the six-foot-high wild ancestor of cattle. The other, which is nearly as old, is much smaller, indicating that its owner was domesticated.

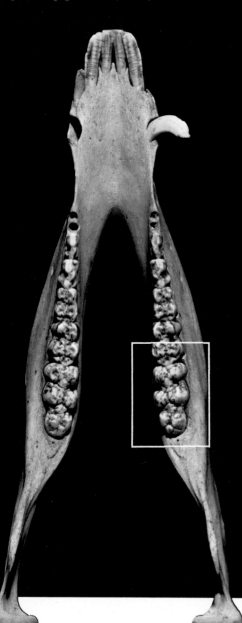

 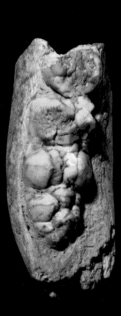

Fragments of two pigs' jawbones from Jarmo, in Iraq, both correspond to the marked part of the jaw at far left. But the one at left belonged to a wild pig, and the fragment at right to a tame one. The latter's jaw was undersized and its teeth crowded, stunting the growth of its third molar (lowest tooth).

The clearest record to date showing the stages of domestication in the early Middle East comes from a low mound called Ali Kosh in Iran near the head of the Persian Gulf. Today Ali Kosh seems hardly fit for occupation by either men or their animals. It stands on a rolling, desolate plain almost devoid of vegetation, ferociously hot in summer, with brackish rivers and sloughs. But in neolithic times, thousands of years before the area was devastated by over-intensive cultivation and overgrazing, Ali Kosh could not have been too bad a place to live. Winter rains were followed by luxuriant bursts of tall spring grasses and flowering plants, the rivers and sloughs were full of fish and migratory waterfowl, and the uplands of near-by mountains offered a cool sanctuary from the blazing summer heat.

Proof that Ali Kosh had indeed been attractive to prehistoric people came in the 1960s, when archaeologists from the United States and Iran excavated the mound and found that it was the site of a village that had been inhabited fairly continuously for about 4,000 years, beginning perhaps as early as 7950 B.C.

The lowest levels yielded remains suggesting that the earliest inhabitants of Ali Kosh were still largely hunter-gatherers. They lived in small, rectangular houses crudely made of sun-dried slabs of mud, and in the refuse around these houses the excavators found many carbonized seeds, mostly of vetch and other wild plants, as well as a few kernels of wheat and barley that, judging by their size, may have been cultivated. The archaeologists also unearthed signs that these hunter-gatherers of nearly 10,000 years ago may already have taken steps towards animal domestication. Among the bones on dumps outside their doors was the skull of a hornless sheep, presumably female, an indication that the inhabitants kept sheep that had begun to show the genetic changes associated with domestication.

Goat bones were much more numerous. Although they were indistinguishable from those of wild goats, most of them belonged to young animals—and this suggested that some sort of selection process was going on. A stronger argument for the goats' domestication came not from the mound itself but from the surrounding plain. Wild goats, whose best defence is their ability to bound up rocky crags where their enemies cannot follow, would normally have avoided such level—and therefore dangerous—country. Their mere presence at Ali Kosh is a pretty good indication that they were brought there from the mountains to enjoy, under watchful eyes, the lush spring grazing of the otherwise perilous plain.

In more recent levels of Ali Kosh the archaeologists found undeniable proof of domestication. Refuse heaps dating from around 6500 B.C. produced horn cores that were beginning to show the oval cross section characteristic of early tame goats. Cores from still-later levels were starting to twist slightly, and ones from about 5000 B.C. were as corkscrew-shaped as those of modern Middle Eastern breeds.

In earlier levels the bones of domesticated sheep were much less numerous, but in later levels they cropped up more and more. How the domesticated breed managed to increase in a region that seems to have been too hot for wild sheep is uncertain. One possibility is that the dense wool coat for which they must have been bred gave them protection against excessive heat. Even wild sheep have a panting mechanism that works like the dog's to keep their bodies cool in summer. By causing evaporation of moisture in the upper respiratory tract it helps reduce the animal's blood temperature. When a sheep is protected from the sun's rays by plenty of wool, this mechanism has less cooling to do, and therefore is more effective.

At Ali Kosh, as elsewhere, domesticated sheep and goats would have been a tremendous asset for neolithic farmers. In the first place, they not only served as handy sources of hide, hair, wool and food but they were to a large extent self-supporting. The farm family could plant its best land with wheat, barley, lentils, peas and other crops, and the animals could graze on land left over because it was too poor, steep or rocky to be cultivated. In effect, they made the farm bigger and more productive.

In addition, goats and sheep are biochemical processing machines that convert materials inedible to man into meat and milk. The sheep could make a living on grain fields after harvest, consuming stubble as well as weeds. The goats could browse on leafy bushes and even climb low trees to nibble twigs. Few mammals can directly digest such marginal plant food; its tissues are made up largely of cellulose, the tough, fibrous and stubbornly insoluble material that contributes structural strength. But sheep and goats are ruminants and have as part of their digestive systems a large pouch, the rumen, where such cellulose-rich food, well-chewed, is attacked by swarming bacteria and other micro-organisms that make part of it soluble and use another part to nourish themselves. The micro-organisms' growth, in turn, is stimulated by urea, a waste in the blood that is recycled into the rumen and helps form protein.

When the contents of the rumen move into the rest of the animal's alimentary canal, both the micro-organisms and the soluble products of the cellulose are digested and used by the animal. This efficient system of utilizing cellulose had made goats, sheep and other ruminants, like cattle, bison and deer, dominant among large plant-eaters, and the ability of man to control and live off the ruminants supports his own dominance of the earth.

Neolithic men, of course, knew nothing about the digestive process of ruminants, but they did know such animals could grow and prosper on foods that human stomachs could not tolerate. When it was discovered that the females, especially goats, could be milked as well, sheep and goats acquired even more vital importance.

Long before they turned from hunting and gathering to farming, the Middle Easterners must have watched with interest lambs and kids being suckled by their mothers. The analogy with their own babies was obvious, so why, they must have wondered, should not humans also benefit from animal milk? Folklore and history are full of instances of humans making use of animal mothers. Romulus and Remus, the legendary founders of Rome, were suckled by a she-wolf. Francisco Pizarro, the Spanish conqueror of Peru, started life as a foundling whose wet nurse was said to be a sow supplied by solicitous nuns.

An advantage of milking is that it provides a way for valuable breeding animals to be productive long before they are eaten. And as soon as men learned to milk their animals into containers, the next step must have followed rapidly. When milk is allowed to sour and stand for a while, it automatically turns into a crude sort of cheese that, after the water or whey is removed, can be cured so that it will stay edible for a long time. The neolithic family whose animals pro-

One of the earliest milking scenes, this impression of a 2500 B.C. Elamite seal depicts a goat being milked in front of the fertility goddess to encourage the animal's productivity.

duced milk and cheese to supplement their supply of vegetable foods thus would have had an almost perfect all-season diet with little need to kill their domestic animals or hunt wild game.

Domesticated sheep and goats eventually spread widely through Asia, Africa and Europe. In the meantime, the Middle East villagers also became the first to tame pigs, and there is a strong possibility that they were the first to have domesticated cattle. Pigs still run wild in the Middle East, as in other parts of Asia and Europe, and their striped piglets are easily tamed. But while there is evidence that pigs may have been domesticated in Middle East villages as early as about 7000 B.C., their remains are fairly scarce in neolithic refuse dumps.

Pigs are not ruminants and therefore cannot efficiently turn coarse vegetable matter into food for man; this may be one reason why they never rivalled goats and sheep in the ancient Middle East. Moreover, many early neolithic villagers may have had an aversion to pigs, abhorring their habit of eating faeces, and perhaps sensing that they could transmit parasitic diseases to humans. Pigs did not become really important livestock until much later, when they began to be bred in primitive villages of Europe and northern China, where they could forage in the forests for food, and where the cooler climate permitted longer and safer meat storage.

Much more important than pigs to early neolithic settlements in the Middle East were cattle. Their domestication, however, seems to have taken place comparatively late. This is understandable, for the now-extinct wild ox, or aurochs, the ancestor of today's domesticated cattle, was a horrendous beast, the well-muscled bulls standing as much as six feet at the shoulders, with long, sharp, businesslike horns and an unpleasant disposition. The cows were smaller, but taking one into the family, so to speak, was quite a different matter from carrying a baby goat or sheep home to tame.

Some authorities believe that the Middle Easterners' first dealing with the aurochs (aside from hunting it) was religious. Since the bull aurochs was the most impressive, vigorous and potentially dangerous animal around, it would have been natural for early neolithic men to adopt it as a symbol of strength and virility. They may even have needed such a symbol because their basic religion appears to have been a "Great Mother" cult, with a woman serving as goddess of procreation. Aurochs' horns were found displayed in shrines at the city of Catal Hüyük in Turkey that date from perhaps as early as 6500 B.C. Well-modelled bulls' heads in plaster protrude from the shrine walls, and figures of the Great Mother herself show her giving birth to a bull.

In this Sumerian frieze of 2500 B.C. the cows still preserve some of the wild look of their progenitor, the aurochs, but submit docilely to milki

Bull worship continued beyond neolithic times, and there are still traces of it today. Egypt of the pharaohs had a bull god, Apis, and bulls were prominent in the religious symbolism of ancient Mesopotamian cities. The Phoenician god Baal was a bull god, and the religion of Minoan Crete included a dangerous ritual of athletes vaulting over the horns of living bulls. Bulls (as well as cows) may have been held sacred in the Indus Valley civilization, just as they are today in modern India; and the Spanish bullfight may be rooted in the bull-vaulting ritual of ancient Crete.

These religious aspects make it difficult to determine when cattle were domesticated for mundane economic purposes. The horns at Catal Hüyük, for instance, may have come from wild bulls killed by hunters, or perhaps from bulls driven into an enclosure and kept there for admiration and eventual sacrifice. On the other hand, cattle bones from refuse heaps at Catal Hüyük pose a mystery. They appear to have come from animals no larger than modern domestic breeds, which are considerably smaller than the wild aurochs. If these were indeed tame animals, then the domestication of cattle was an accomplished fact in Turkey about 8,000 years ago. But there is another possibility—and it is that the bones may have come from small wild cattle. The aurochs was a widespread and highly variable species, and a strain no larger than modern cattle may have lived in Turkey.

Some archaeologists have begun to claim that cattle were first domesticated not in the Middle East but in Greece, perhaps as early as 6200 B.C. The evidence they offer are bones discovered in the 1960s at Nea Nikomedeia, a neolithic village in northern Greece. Representing mostly immature animals, the bones

the left of the gateway, milk is being strained, and heavy cream, contained in a large jug, is then rocked back and forth to produce butter.

could be from cattle selected for slaughter from domesticated herds.

Whether it first happened in Greece or, as seems more likely, in the Middle East, the fierce aurochs was turned into a more placid animal. In some breeds the horns grew smaller or actually disappeared. In other breeds, which were developed more for show than utility, the horns became larger. Dwarf cattle appeared, and cattle of every colour that mammals can exhibit. But the ancestor of them all, the wild aurochs, eventually became extinct; the last known survivor was killed in Poland in 1627.

However, because some modern breeds are still fairly aurochs-like, European zoologists were able to pull off a genetic tour de force and create "bred-back" animals that are believed to closely resemble the ancestral stock. When cattle possessing different assort-

ments of aurochs genes were mated, some of their offspring acquired more of these genes than either parent had. When the offspring in turn were selected for breeding, and this procedure was repeated several times, an aurochs-like animal began to emerge. The re-created wild cattle are not so large as the original aurochs, but they do look like 17th Century pictures of it and they have its celebrated courage, nasty disposition and fast footwork. They illustrate plainly why cattle were not the first animals to join man's entourage.

With the addition of cattle, the early villagers of the Middle East had their basic set of farm animals. In time—and elsewhere—other animals were tamed. Horses, domesticated somewhere in southwestern Russia around 3000 B.C., arrived in the Middle East about 2500 B.C., after true civilization had risen there.

Breeding the Many Varieties of Domesticated Dogs

A squat, hairless dog was bred in Mexico.

Only a thin thread of fossil evidence links the first domesticated dogs of the early farmers to their wild forebear the wolf. But ancient artifacts like those shown here from all over the world suggest that dog breeding by the early farmers soon produced distinct varieties, with traits specially desirable for herding, hunting or guarding. In fact, all of the main types of dog known today had been developed—and were widely dispersed—by the dawn of recorded history.

Egyptian aristocrats, who hunted for sport at a very early date, took pride in breeding and following swift, keen-eyed hounds (*right*). The Assyrians, breeding for size and ferocity, developed giant mastiffs to hunt by scent and to attack big game and human enemies. Smaller dogs served everywhere as village scavengers and ratters but were especially esteemed at opposite ends of the ancient world. In China the tiny Pekingese became a pampered symbol of wealth and refinement, while in Mexico the Aztec Indians bred even smaller species for ritual sacrifices and for food.

Predecessors of the greyhound display their prowess in a drawing of an Egyptian relief. Four scenes show they were fleet enough to catch gazelles, strong enough to bring down ibexes, daring enough to attack wild cattle, bristling hedgehogs and snapping geese.

A lion-hunting mastiff follows the scent in an Assyrian relief.

Tiny and smug, a Chinese pet fits into a bowl-like bed.

They were about the same size as an onager or wild ass, and at first their principal use was to draw carts and war chariots. Soon, however, they were being bred to make them bigger, and by 1500 B.C. horses had been developed that were big enough for a man to ride. Camels, useful mainly for transport, were first tamed around 3000 B.C. in Central Asia. But neither of these animals had an economic effect comparable to that of sheep, goats and cattle.

Curiously, the rest of the world's contribution to man's barnyard was small. The chicken was domesticated in India around 2000 B.C. and did not become widespread until Greek and Roman times. In ancient Peru the most important meat producers were guinea pigs, famous for their rapid reproduction. The Peruvians also domesticated the guanaco, a donkey-sized ruminant related to the camel, and by selective breeding turned it into two useful forms, the llama and the alpaca. Both were eaten, as they still are in Peru, but since they bred and grew slowly the llama became chiefly a pack animal, while the alpaca was valued primarily for its fine wool.

In Central America the early farmers had a wider selection of possible domesticates. The bighorn sheep was native to northern Mexico, and so was the bison, which is a close relative of cattle and is certainly no more obstreperous than the aurochs. But the Mexicans—and the Indians farther to the north—apparently made no attempt to domesticate them. The Mexicans' contribution was the turkey, although in prehistoric America the Thanksgiving bird was never a major source of food.

It is interesting to speculate what might have happened if the Aztecs or the other civilized people of southern Mexico had domesticated the bighorn sheep or bison. They would almost certainly have spread in force over northern Mexico, which is excellent grazing country. Given a thousand years of animal husbandry before the Spanish conquerors arrived, herds of bison and their herdsmen might have occupied the grassland parts of the United States.

The animals so far described were generally important as ready-to-hand, dependable sources of food. But two of the animals most intimately associated with man—the dog and the cat—had no more economic significance in most parts of the prehistoric world than they do today. In fact, the common house cat has left no record of its having been domesticated before the dawn of history. The earliest, though inconclusive, evidence for its domestication comes from Egypt in about 3000 B.C., where it presumably descended from small wild cats that hung around human settlements to prey on the rodents that infested refuse dumps and granaries. Certainly by 1400 B.C. cats were held in high esteem by the Egyptians, who worshipped them as sacred to the cat-headed goddess Bastet. But the common mouse-catcher of ancient Egypt was not the cat—it was the house snake. Similarly, the cat may have been surpassed as a rat-catcher in Sumer by the mongoose: a common adage put it this way: "A cat—for its thoughts! A mongoose —for its deeds!"

The first of man's household pets probably was the dog. It is believed by some even to antedate domesticated goats and sheep by thousands of years. But not all archaeologists accept the dog's claim to such great antiquity, and this lack of agreement is further confused by nonexperts who look on dogs sentimentally and insist on their being honoured as "man's oldest friend".

There is not much evidence to support either side of the argument. Dog bones rarely turn up in neolithic refuse heaps along with the well-picked bones of sheep and goats. This may be partly because dogs, unlike these and other ruminants, compete for food that man himself can eat directly. Therefore they would have been few.

Another reason for the scarcity of dog bones is that in most parts of the ancient world dogs seem to have been eaten only out of dire necessity. (A notable exception is prehistoric Mexico, where small dogs were purposely fattened to eat.) It is pleasant to think that when a dog died, its master buried it with honours outside the village, but more likely he tossed its body aside where the vultures and other scavengers tore it to bits and scattered the bones.

Not only are dog bones scarce at ancient sites, but they are often very much like the bones of wolves and such other dog-like wild animals as the jackal. Before domestication had wrought conspicuous changes, the differences between wolf and dog skeletons were slight. Early dog skulls often have muzzles shorter than those of typical wolves. Some dogs' teeth are crowded together, but this too is a peculiarity that some wolves share.

The earliest remains considered to be those of domesticated dogs have an odd geographical distribution. The oldest came from human debris in Idaho and were radiocarbon dated at about 9000 B.C. The next oldest, dating from 7500 B.C., were found in northern England. In the Middle East, which for a long time was presumed to be the centre of dog domestication, the first dog bones date from about 7000 B.C.

These scattered finds may indicate that dogs were first domesticated in some unknown place in very ancient times, perhaps before the end of the ice age, and then spread from this source. Or it may mean that dogs were domesticated many times in different places, just as agriculture itself was reinvented around the world. On the other hand, a figurine found during Robert Braidwood's excavations at Jarmo shows a low-slung dog very much like a Scottish terrier with its tail curled over its back, a non-wolf-like trait. If the 6700 B.C. figurine really represents a dog and not some product of the artist's imagination, it indicates that Jarmo dogs must have had plenty of time to diverge from the original wolf-like model.

Perhaps the answer to the puzzling distribution of early dog remains—as well as an explanation of how dogs became domesticated in the first place—can be found in the widespread range of wolves and in their strong social life. Many wolf races and subspecies differing widely in size and colour are scattered over the earth, and all live in tight groups. These packs, which are often no more than a single family, but may consist of a dozen or more members, have recognized leaders and share food with one another. They hunt co-operatively and are therefore able to bring down game too large and dangerous for a single wolf to handle. Their organization sounds like that of primitive men, and it is indeed similar. Since wolves are social animals, individuals do not act independently but as members of groups.

Such being the case, it is extremely easy to tame a captured wolf pup. It is an adorable ball of fluff, full of playfulness and affection, and it quickly attaches itself to the human beings who care for it, substituting them for its own family and pack.

Since taming wolves is so easy, it may have been done over and over again, beginning tens of thousands of years ago. And the tamed wolves—on the way to becoming dogs—may have died out repeatedly after a few generations for want of economic function. In theory they may have been useful to preagricultural people as aids in hunting, but there is no archaeological proof of this, and few contemporary hunter-gatherers hunt with dogs. Dogs may have increased in importance only after neolithic men had domesticated sheep and goats and needed them to help herd and protect the flocks against predators, and to give warning of the approach of strangers. Certainly this is the most important economic use of dogs in modern times, but whether neolithic villagers used them in such a way can only be conjectured.

Nevertheless, dogs no doubt were useful in other minor ways to neolithic people. The prehistoric North American Indians, for example, are known to have tolerated dogs as scavengers around their camps and settlements, which usually needed such policing. Dogs were also useful to chase away wild animals. On the plains of the West they served to carry or drag light loads when it came time to break camp and move to a new location; and the Eskimos used dogs to pull sledges, although this is an innovation that is thought to be relatively recent. Duties like these, however, were not essential to early neolithic life, so it seems unlikely that determined efforts were made to raise and keep tame dogs; they could always be re-domesticated from the local stock of wolves. Such multiple domestication during long ages and in many parts of the world may account for the innumerable, widely differing breeds of dogs that appear to have their origin deep in prehistory.

Chapter Five: The Security of Village Life

Both right side up and upside down, this 5650 B.C. cup from the Turkish farming village of Hacilar is believed to have been a ceremonial object. As a cup (above), it was probably used to pour libations. When turned over (right), it became a stylized figurine of a woman's head, with incised eyes and a protruding nose. The sophisticated dual-purpose design, appearing only a century after pottery making began at Hacilar, points up the rapid progress made by the skilled local craftsmen.

From neolithic times until the beginning of the modern industrial age most people lived in farming villages. Their food came from surrounding fields and pastures, and whatever else they needed they made for themselves out of raw materials nature provided. They found in villages the security and companionship they needed. Everyone knew everyone. Skills could be exchanged. Harvesting the crops and other heavy tasks could be lightened by co-operative effort, and the near-by graves of ancestors gave a comforting sense of belonging and continuity.

The vital human institution of the farm village originated independently in various parts of the prehistoric world and at various times. But its beginnings are best understood in the Middle East, where the world's first farming villages appeared around 7000 B.C., with roots reaching back to the dim days before agriculture when the only people on earth were nomadic hunter-gatherers.

Once archaeologists became interested in the neolithic revolution as a giant step towards civilization, they started to excavate some of these earliest villages and to piece together a fascinating and largely unknown chapter in the story of human progress. Here were the rudimentary beginnings of architecture, however humble the buildings themselves, most of which were mud-walled or crude stone houses. The construction and arrangement of these early abodes also provided clues to man's social organization after he began to settle down. In the tools, ornaments and other artifacts unearthed within the villages could be read the trend towards specialized skills and crafts that sedentary living encouraged. Clay and stone figurines that seem to have had a sacred meaning and plain structures that may represent shrines suggested emerging religious beliefs.

In a good many of the settlements, archaeologists came upon remains of houses that could not have been strikingly different from those seen in some parts of the Middle East today. They were rectangular, mud-walled structures clustered closely together with common outer walls and several rooms each. But in a few unusually old settlements that were primitive even by prehistoric standards, a different kind of architecture showed up: round houses. These were indicated by circles of stones that apparently had reinforced a pole framework that must have been covered with hides or some other perishable material that disappeared long ago. The huts often stood separate, with a good deal of space between them, and in a couple of instances they were arranged in an oval or in a circle. They may well represent man's first permanent dwellings outside caves.

The change-over in some villages from small, round huts to rectangular houses huddled together gives rise to a tantalizing question. Does the shift reflect nothing more than the adoption of mud as a building material, or does it reveal something basic about the establishment of settled society made possible by farming?

One widely respected theorist, Kent V. Flannery of the University of Michigan, points out that round huts are favoured by many modern primitives, especially those who move from place to place a good deal, because they are relatively easy to build. A few poles, with the larger ends placed in a circle and with their top ends leaning inwards and fastened together, make a quickly erected frame that can be covered with skins, leaves or thatch. A hut built on this simple plan supports itself firmly, and it can be made portable like the tepees of the Indians on the American plains. Flannery suggests that the nomadic hunters who were the ancestors of the first Middle East villagers may have constructed shelters this way, and their descendants who took to the settled life simply continued the old tradition.

But why should the huts of a permanent settlement be small? Some found in Israel are less than nine feet in diameter, a space in which even a tepee-dwelling Indian family would have felt badly crowded. That they were indeed human habitations and not merely storage places or shelters for domestic animals is proved by the presence inside of hearths and stones for grinding grain. But as quarters for a family they appear unnecessarily cramped.

Here again Flannery suggests an answer based on observations of existing primitives. Among some of these the biological family—a man, his wife and his unmarried children—is not always the most important grouping, as it is in most modern societies. The same may have been true in the very ancient Middle East. In many parts of sub-Saharan Africa, where tribesmen like the Massa people of Cameroun still live on an early neolithic cultural level, the basic social and economic unit also includes a man's married sons, their wives and their offspring, who share both the work and the benefits of such an arrangement. This emphasis on the extended family is reflected in both the dwellings the people live in and their layout. Most huts are quite small, and many are only a foot or so greater in diameter than those that were unearthed in Israel. One man or one woman (with or without small children) sleeps in each of the smaller shelters. The larger ones may accommodate a man and two cows or a woman and several goats. Along

with adjacent kitchen huts and granaries the huts are often erected in a circle, with those of the men and women usually on opposite sides, no matter who is married to whom.

This arrangement, which is shared with small differences by many other African tribes today, may seem contrary to human nature—but then it is all a matter of cultural conditioning. To most Americans it seems natural that a man and his wife should want to live together and keep their children near by without too much crowding. But the inhabitants of these modern circular villages do not feel this way at all. They are communalists with little feeling for personal property, except weapons, clothing and other personal effects, and with a strong tradition of sharing. Even the headman's large granary is regarded as a reserve that all may draw on in time of need. The small huts arranged in a circle without concern for family grouping are an architectural expression of this all-are-equal attitude.

The circular compounds of modern Africa are not necessarily related to the round-hut villages of the ancient Middle East, but similar social forces may have been at work in the Middle East 10,000 years ago. Indeed, both types of villages may go back to nomadic hunter-gatherers who laid out their first settlements according to plans that reflected their social customs. In Africa this communalism is still alive and still building its egalitarian villages. But in the Middle East it apparently did not long survive the change from nomadic to settled village life.

When the nomads learned how to collect food so efficiently that they could settle down permanently, and their descendants in turn learned how to produce food by farming, the social imperatives seem to have changed. The evidence for this is a proliferation of personal property, brought to light by archaeologists digging up the remains of early villages. The settled life encouraged this trend. Items too heavy for nomads to carry from camp to camp no longer had to be abandoned. A woman could keep her favourite grinding stones. A man could accumulate a large assortment of weapons, hunting equipment and livestock. Some foods could be stored for long periods, giving insurance against times of scarcity. More possessions called for bigger houses, and privately accumulated stocks of food weakened the traditional custom of share and share alike.

The Middle Easterners' shift away from communal living probably took centuries at least. In some places round, stone-based huts began to be built in small clusters, suggesting that the more industrious and ambitious individuals were getting away from the tradition of isolated huts and approaching the idea of building comfortable, multiroomed structures to house each family under one roof. Once this step was taken, it no doubt seemed more practical to build rectangular houses.

A single rectangular room, perhaps divided by partitions, could accommodate a medium-sized family and, if not, additional rooms could be added by using existing walls as parts of the new structure. The growing house might extend around a courtyard where the family could work or keep their animals. Since the house was rectangular its roof could be flat, and, reached by stairs or a ladder, it more than likely provided a pleasant, semiprivate place for the family's enjoyment; flat roofs are still used that way in Middle Eastern countries, where people sleep on them during warm weather.

Architectural Keys to Social Change
Reflecting social development, the village of Beidha, in Jordan, underwent radical changes in architecture in 500 years. In these diagrams of the houses from two layers half a millennium apart, the round dwellings of 7000 B.C. (*above*) were built in clusters (1), with storage areas near by (2). All occupants of each cluster may have been related; they lived one or two per hut. The later houses were rectangular, and families apparently lived together under one roof. In the unit diagrammed below, living quarters were presumably on the second stories of shops (3), near a meeting house (4) and a courtyard (5).

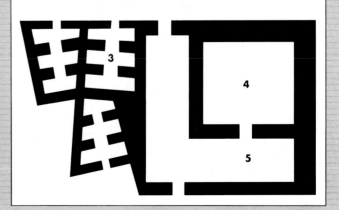

It is too much to say that the appearance in the Middle East of rectangular houses of several rooms marked precisely the shift from communalism to village life. The transition was halting and ragged. Villages have been uncovered with small round dwellings existing contemporaneously with larger rectangular ones. No doubt there were endless and bitter recriminations, with traditionalists denouncing those selfish families that were slighting their community duties to accumulate personal property for their own use. No doubt some aspects of the old-time egalitarian system, such as sharing food in time of famine, had social value that tended to keep such aspects of it alive. However this went, men eventually came to live with their wives and children in multiroomed, rectangular houses, as they do today, and to think of their families as their first obligation.

This evolution of house architecture can be traced, along with the development of villages themselves, in a number of recently excavated Middle East sites. But building styles were not uniform, even over comparatively small areas. Often advanced details appear in one village but not in others near by that date from the same period, and in some villages rectangular houses are later superseded by small round huts in the archaic style. In a world without any means of transport there could not have been much communication between villages more than a few miles apart, and there may even have been hostility. Differences of language may also have kept people separate by preventing ideas and fashions from spreading fast or far. One archaeological site that spans the entire fascinating evolution of the neolithic village and its houses—from the camp of hunter-gatherers to the fully-fledged farming settlement—is Beidha, in Jordan, about 30 miles southeast of the Dead Sea. Its seven levels of human occupation were meticulously excavated in the 1960s by British archaeologists. The leader of the dig, Diana Kirkbride of Oxford University, described their findings in the December 1968 issue of *Antiquity*.

The site stands on a sandy terrace overlooking a desert-floored valley on the west. It is separated from the Arabian Desert on the east by a low range of sandstone mountains. The country around it is desolate now, but in 8000 B.C. or so it must have looked like a promised land. Botanical studies show that an open forest of oak, pistachio, wild fig, almond and juniper flourished on the slopes, and zoologists have identified the bones of many kinds of edible wild animals —among them those of goats, pigs, gazelles, aurochs and onagers or asses. The rainfall too may have been somewhat greater then than it is today, and an undisturbed cover of vegetation would have helped to keep the water table high.

Into this pleasant country, some time before 7500 B.C., came Beidha's first occupants, a band of hunter-gatherers who camped on the high terrace from which they could watch the valley below for prey and perhaps enemies. Their camp may have been seasonal only, but, judging from the quantity of debris they left, they must have returned to it repeatedly. They also left traces of two extremely simple structures. One, a circular, stone-floored pit, is presumably the foundation of a semisubterranean hut; the other is a circular clay floor that may have been covered by a tepee-like shelter.

Housing, obviously, did not mean much to those hardy people, but they made themselves comfortable in other ways. Around a circular hearth more than three feet in diameter were sandstone slabs, some with bones still on them; these must have been used as dining tables to keep the food cooked there free of sand. Such graphic evidence makes it easy to imagine the people themselves sitting around the low slabs toasting strips of meat in the flames of the hearth or perhaps hacking at haunches or whole animals that had been buried in hot coals to bake.

Other evidence carefully sifted from the debris of Beidha tells more about how these hunter-gatherers lived. Spear points and scrapers and some stone chips indicate that flint was their major material for tool-making. A few tusk-shaped dentalia shells, highly prized as ornaments in the prehistoric Middle East and perhaps fallen from a woman's broken necklace, suggest hand-to-hand trade with the Mediterranean coast 95 miles away.

Around 7500 B.C. the hunter-gatherers left Beidha; perhaps they killed most of the game. The site was unoccupied long enough for it to be buried, and then around 7000 B.C. fresh arrivals moved in. The newcomers were still primitive, but in some respects they were more advanced than their predecessors had been. For one thing they brought with them the magic knowledge of agriculture. Very likely they had sent scouts ahead to look for water and fertile land, after which they trooped up to Beidha carrying their most precious possessions, the keys to their life —baskets of wheat and barley with which to plant their new crops. These incipient farmers, distinguished as the people of Level VI by Beidha's excavators, come into sharper focus than do the transient hunter-gatherers. They were, in a sense, pioneers, and their first effort seems to have been to erect temporary shelters on the clay floors. Postholes

left in the ground indicate that these shelters may have consisted merely of poles supporting some kind of light roof. The settlers also built sunken hearths, one of which was surrounded by a rim of clay bricks, apparently placed there to keep out shifting sand.

Having made themselves at home and perhaps having planted their first crops, these pioneers turned to building permanent, partially subterranean houses. They seem to have known just what to do, and their relatively advanced architecture suggests that they were already heirs to a tradition brought with them from no one knows where. First they dug circular pits in the sand about a foot and a half deep and 12 feet in diameter, and lined them with stones from the near-by mountains and dry streambeds. In a generally arid country like Jordan, houses built partially below ground level do not suffer from dampness; they are easy to keep warm, and the undisturbed soil helps support the walls.

Above each of these stone-lined pits, these early farmers erected a framework of posts, like the vertical studs of a modern wood frame house, and connected the tops by beams to a stouter post set in the centre of the floor, which was then finished in a sandy textured plaster. A stone wall, also plastered, was constructed around this inner skeleton, and the whole was covered by poles, brush and reeds topped with a thick layer of clay to form a roof sufficiently waterproof to keep out the infrequent rains. Each house was entered by stone steps through an opening in the side wall.

These small round structures were arranged in clusters, like the cells in a honeycomb, the houses touching wherever they converged. Obviously the builders did not trust their masonry walls to stand

Substitute Mothers for the Journey Beyond the Grave

These eerie-eyed, plump female statuettes of alabaster, unearthed at the town of Tell es-Sawwan in Iraq and dated back to 6000 B.C., have inspired speculation about the early art and religion of the first farming villages. Stylistically, the eyes of inlaid shell, with painted pupils and eyebrows, closely resemble—and possibly influenced—the large, staring eyes of votive figures carved in stone three millennia later in the cities of Sumer.

But the statuettes' purpose was religious rather than artistic. In fact, most of the two dozen figures were found in the graves of children. This has suggested to archaeologists that the statuettes may have been placed there as substitutes for the real mothers to comfort the helpless youngsters on their journey to the unknown.

Fifteen female figurines, many with their arms clasped in front of them, are assumed to have been surrogate mothers. All of them appear to be naked, a few with necklaces and some with their hair piled on top of their heads.

firm, even though these were reinforced by a wooden frame; the interstices were filled with stones or smaller structures, such as storage bins for holding grain or other foodstuffs. Anterooms or short corridors connected the houses of each cluster, and the clusters themselves were surrounded by stone walls.

Unluckily for the farmers of Beidha but luckily for archaeologists, the Level VI settlement caught fire and burned fiercely because of the large amount of wood in the buildings. The mud-coated roofs fell, covering the houses' contents and preserving an extraordinary assortment of articles.

Fragments of bone and carbonized vegetable remains provided plentiful clues to the economy of the ancient villagers. The seed wheat they had brought with them was emmer, partly the easily shattered variety and partly the domesticated nonshattering kind. Their barley was all of the wild type; some of it may have been gathered from wild stands. In addition, they collected wild leguminous seeds, such as lentils and peas, and these added protein to their diet. They herded domesticated goats but also hunted wild animals. This adds up to an early and primitive kind of agricultural life, but in other ways the villagers were not so primitive.

When the British diggers finished clearing the charred ruins, they had amassed a rich inventory —not only of the foods the villagers had eaten but also of many articles they had used in their daily life. Some of the small round rooms seem to have been workshops showing the beginnings of specialized skills and crafts. One shop contained mostly large, heavy stone objects such as mortars, pestles and other apparatus for grinding grain or seeds. Another featured boneworking and had a supply of bones and horns as raw material. It was also apparently something of a paint shop; lumps of ochre, malachite and other bright-coloured materials for making pigments were still on the premises.

The most interesting shop belonged to a master craftsman whose facilities included eight large flat stones that apparently served as workbenches for polishing stone and bone artifacts. Their surfaces were finely polished as though from constant use, and scattered about were pieces of pumice and other abrasive and polishing materials. Even more exciting finds turned up here. One consisted of two small, round baskets and a fragment of a third, the earliest baskets yet found anywhere in the world. Another was a wooden box—represented only by a "shadow" of contrasting colour left in the earth after the wood disintegrated—that contained 114 flint spear or arrow points. Although they were beautifully made, they were not quite finished. Evidently the shop's owner did not have time to complete them before fire swept and destroyed the village.

Beidha was rebuilt after the fire and soon rebuilt again after what may have been an earthquake. There was not much change in its agriculture or general way of life, but its architecture showed signs of slowly moving away from the ancient pattern of clusters of small round huts. Some of the later houses were free-standing, and more or less rectangular—but they had curving walls and rounded corners. While their builders apparently were still affected by the old round-hut tradition, they seem to have recognized the advantages of the rectangular plan. They had also gained confidence in their construction techniques and omitted the wooden posts that had reinforced the walls of Level VI houses.

With the people of Level IV, around 6800 B.C., come the first hints of different social levels at Beidha. Three large rectangular houses measuring 16 by 20 feet displayed interiors finely finished in plaster, equipped with hearths bordered by plastered sills. Set into the sills were stone bowls; food could have been boiled in the bowls by filling them with water and then dropping hot stones into them. These houses faced a large open space, like the central plaza of a Latin American town. Around them and across the plaza were much smaller rectangular houses.

The big houses may have belonged to leading families that bossed a population of artisans and farmers. If so, Beidha had taken only about 200 years to change from an egalitarian community, with rights inherited from seminomadic ancestors, to a stratified social structure dominated by a few rich individuals —a remarkable evolution.

Again the village was levelled twice, perhaps by earthquakes, and rebuilt. Many novel features suggest that new people may have moved in. The village plan became almost gridlike, and by the time of the Level II people, about 6600 B.C., Beidha was dominated by a house 23 by 30 feet, whose single large room was finished inside with burnished whitish plaster. Wide bands of red paint, which may have been applied when the plaster was still fresh as in more modern frescoes, covered the walls from the base to the ceiling. Similar bands outlined the hearth —a seat or table of polished stone and a stone-lined pit with a large boulder in its bottom.

Outside this rather imposing structure stretched open courtyards, and beyond them an array of rectangular buildings in even rows. Each consisted of thick stone walls enclosing six small, cubicle-like rooms and a central corridor. Some of the cubicles may have been storerooms, but others were obviously workshops. They were as cramped as the artisans' niches in modern Middle East bazaars, and a great deal more developed than the workshops of Level VI. To judge from articles left in them, some of their proprietors were specialists in different kinds of stone, bone or horn work. One was a jeweller who made stone beads; another cut beads out of hollow bones. One shop with many animal bones and horned skulls may have housed a butcher, or possibly a supplier of bones and horns to other workers. Where the workers themselves lived is in doubt, for the tiny cubicles contained no hearths or other equipment necessary for carrying on daily life. The walls of the cubicles are thick; they may have supported a long-vanished upper storey used for living quarters. In any event, Beidha by 6500 B.C. seems to have been not only a farming village but a rural industrial centre as well, supplying other villages with goods of its own manufacture and dominated by a management group whose headquarters may have been the large building with its red-banded walls and floor.

But Beidha's days were numbered. Since the first farmers moved in about 7000 B.C., the village had grown successively smaller, perhaps because reckless cultivation and grazing had robbed the land around of its fertility. The site was abandoned about 6500 B.C. and was not reoccupied until several centuries before Christ, when a Semitic people called Nabataeans installed elaborate water-controlling systems and made its soil productive again. This renaissance, known as Level I, did not endure, however. At present, the Beidha region has no inhabitants except wandering Bedouins.

Other settlements that flourished in roughly the same period as Beidha, but in better-watered, more fertile land, enjoyed a richer and pleasanter life. The first early agricultural village to be excavated was Jarmo, in the hill country of northeastern Iraq. It could not have looked very different from many modern Middle East villages, with its rectangular houses constructed of *tauf*, an Arabic word for building material still employed in the Middle East. The builder first lays a foundation of good-sized stones; then he mixes a clayey mud with water to a consistency that will stand alone, and tempers it with straw to prevent cracking. He moulds a wall on its foundation to a height of three or four inches and lets it dry in the sun while he works on another wall. Course after course is added until all the walls of the houses reach the desired height. This is a slow but not bad way to build. A *tauf* wall is a monolith without the weakness sometimes caused by badly laid bricks.

A typical Jarmo house of 6700 B.C. had a long, rectangular main room, 18 by 7 feet, divided transversely by a *tauf* partition that may not have reached the roof. The two sections were living and sleeping quarters. Beside them was another room of about the same size, divided into four small storage spaces. A hallway led past the end of the storage room to an open walled courtyard, which was probably used for grinding grain and other household tasks and penning animals. The floors of the roofed-over rooms were covered with reed matting—this is known because the matting left an imprint on the underlying mud. In its prime, Jarmo probably had about 25 such houses with alleys or courtyards between them.

Two surprisingly sophisticated features for such ancient times were Jarmo's doors and ovens. The

Harvest time in a Fortified Village

Harvest time for the 100-odd people who lived in the Turkish village of Hacilar about 5400 B.C. meant long, hot days of toil. Their activities, as well as the buildings they lived in, are reconstructed at right in a painting based on British archaeologist James Mellaart's excavation of the site.

The scene takes place in late afternoon. From outside the four-foot-thick walls, workers bring sacks of wheat and barley through the northwest gate (3) into the north courtyard (4). There a woman parches the grain in an oven (5) so husks can be stripped off before the seeds are stored in the granary (6). On top of the two-storey house next door (7) other women are drying fruit; two pause on the roof below for a bite of bread. Still others are preparing meals (8) beside the kitchens (9) near the east wall (2). At the south gate (10), boys herd the village flock to nighttime safety in the south courtyard (11), where milking is underway. In a partitioned area close by (12), a couple weave baskets. Diagonally across from them, in the yards next to the pottery workshops (13), potters paint and dry their wares. Beyond the workshops stands a shrine (15), which two worshippers enter carrying bundled offerings. To the right of the shrine is the well (16), where villagers are drawing water. Children without specific chores are seen playing on the roofs and on top of Hacilar's wall.

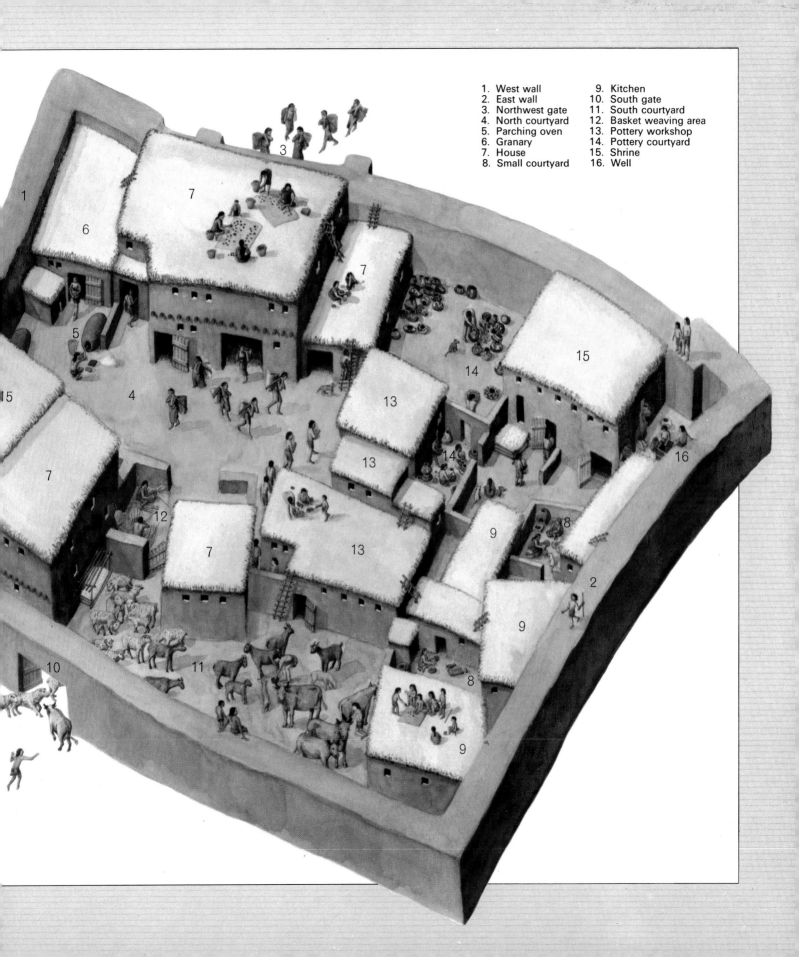

1. West wall
2. East wall
3. Northwest gate
4. North courtyard
5. Parching oven
6. Granary
7. House
8. Small courtyard
9. Kitchen
10. South gate
11. South courtyard
12. Basket weaving area
13. Pottery workshop
14. Pottery courtyard
15. Shrine
16. Well

doors themselves long ago disappeared—presumably they were made of wood—but their "hinges" show how they worked. Set into the floor and wall at the top and bottom of the hinge side of the doorway were stones with round sockets. Into these fitted the ends of a round-ended doorpost. Such a door may have squeaked as the doorpost turned in the stone socket, but when closed by a simple bolt or bar it was strong enough to keep out intruders. Obviously the people of Jarmo valued their privacy and property and took pains to preserve both.

The Jarmo oven consisted of a dome of *tauf* built inside one of the storage spaces. Its fire door opened on the courtyard and its flue ran up the wall and presumably ended in a chimney above the roof. This sort of oven is still in use in many parts of the world. Indeed it was not different in principle from the brick ovens of colonial New England. Its operation was simple and effective. Fuel was stoked through the fire door, and the fire was allowed to burn until the inside of the oven was as hot as desired. The coals and ashes were then raked out and food put in. The fire door was closed, and the food was left to be cooked by the radiating heat from the oven walls. The Jarmo oven may also have been used to heat grain, so as to loosen the husks and make the seeds easier to grind. Temperatures could be kept below the burning point, and the oven had the advantage, which open fires lack, of heating food on all sides.

The incongruously advanced doors and ovens of Jarmo are only one illustration of the surprising finds that frequently confront archaeologists exploring the remains of very early Middle East villages. Among other sites that produced the unexpected was Ganj-Dareh in western Iran. Not only did the earliest proof of animal domestication turn up here in the form of hoofprints in clay, but also evidence that by 7000 B.C. the villagers were living in complicated two-storey houses. This find did not announce itself all at once. The diggers first came upon puzzling clusters of cubicles too small for anyone to live in. The thick walls were made of round-topped mud bricks, some of them three feet long, laid in mud mortar. There were no doors or windows, although some of the cubicles had small portholes that could be closed with clay discs or cones. Many were furnished with bins or alcoves. One of the cubicles contained a niche with the skulls of two wild sheep set one above the other; this may have been a shrine before which Ganj-Dareh's hunters prayed before a hunt began. But how did the worshippers get into the shrine?

When the archaeologists got around to excavating them fully, the mystery of the doorless, windowless cubicles was solved. Only then did the diggers realize that these were small basement rooms supporting an upper storey and that they probably had been entered from above. Although the village had burned, traces were found in the ruins of beams that had supported the floors where the people lived; there also were remnants of the beams and canes that had supported a roof of mud. Most of the small basement rooms probably were used for storage. No trace of grain or other stored material remained, but several large stone mortars suggested that wheat or barley was dehulled or ground there.

Cayönü, a village of incipient farmers in the foothills of the Taurus Mountains of southern Turkey, also yielded its share of surprises. Its inhabitants, who settled the site as hunter-gatherers not long be-

Text continued on page 111

Stylized Patterns in Peasant Pottery

Some of the most attractive pottery made by prehistoric men came from the Turkish farming village of Hacilar. The Hacilar potters started out with two local assets: a source of fine-textured clay, and a craft tradition that was already old when they made their first vessels around 5750 B.C. To this heritage they added their own unique blend of skill, imagination and taste; and for more than half a millennium, until fire damaged their village irreparably, they produced the striking pottery designs sampled on these pages.

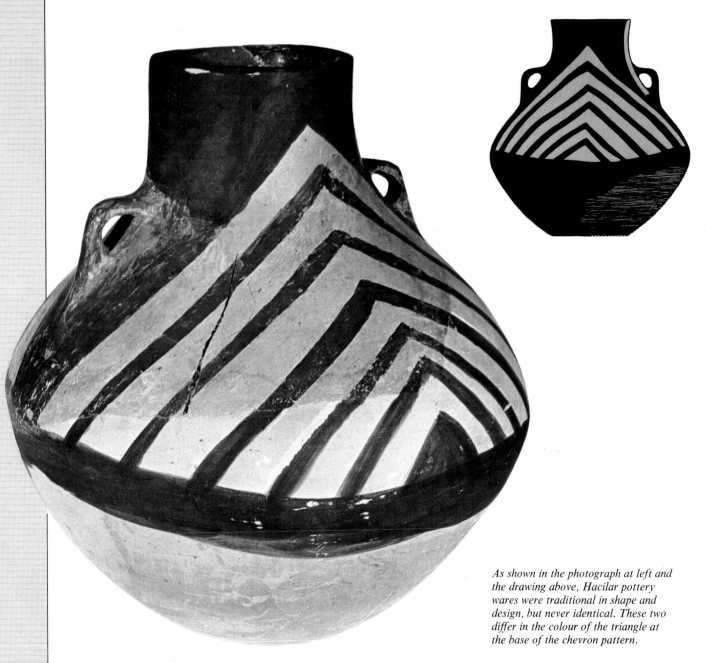

As shown in the photograph at left and the drawing above, Hacilar pottery wares were traditional in shape and design, but never identical. These two differ in the colour of the triangle at the base of the chevron pattern.

Picasso-like Religious Designs

Human and animal patterns decorate all of the Hacilar vessels shown here —though the modern viewer would scarcely know it at first glance. According to the excavator of Hacilar, archaeologist James Mellaart, the goddess of fertility was symbolized by a steplike design (right and below). The goddess' male counterpart was represented by a big-horned bull, and her all-seeing power by an eye design. The four-fingered hands may have been intended for protection against evil.

The designs on these three bowls are symbols for the goddess of fertility. The steps represent profiles of the seated goddess' head, breasts and knees. On the largest bowl the goddess is flanked by stylized animals.

The bull, male symbol of fertility, is represented by the head and horns in the jug above. Four bulls' heads appear in yellow in the bowl at right, their outlines formed by the dark design.

The mother goddess' all-seeing eyes decorate these three vessels. Two of the pots are upside down; they appear to have been designed to be turned over after use, thus strengthening the impression of a woman's head.

Designs showing hands with three or four fingers may have been intended to ward off evil spirits. A three-fingered gesture is still widely used in the Mediterranean area for that purpose.

Patterns from the Everyday World
The world around them inspired Hacilar's potters to make many of their dramatic decorations. Their sources included the woven patterns of baskets and textiles. Flowers were also a popular motif, perhaps as a symbol of fruition. The four-petalled floral motif almost always resembles a Maltese cross. But a few flower-like designs —one appears on the bowl directly below—are so fancifully embellished that they defy positive interpretation.

Floral designs

Basketry patterns

Textile motif

fore 7000 B.C., seem to have been remarkably open to new ideas. They soon acquired domesticated sheep, goats and pigs whose bones were found mingled with those of wild deer and cattle. They eventually mastered plant cultivation as well. And while they were busy at these revolutionary changes in life style, one of their house builders produced a startling triumph for his day: a terrazzo floor made of limestone chips mixed with a hard concrete-like binder. Embedded in the surface were small salmon-pink pebbles set off by two parallel bands of white pebbles. After the binder had set, the pebbles were ground flat and the whole surface was polished. Except for the help of mechanical grinders, this is the way terrazzo floors are made today.

A terrazzo floor in a crude, 9,000-year-old farming-village house was indeed unexpected, but Cayönü held still another surprise. About 12 miles away is a copper deposit that is still being worked. In neolithic time it was a source of malachite, a bright-green copper ore that made colourful ornaments. The alert craftsmen of Cayönü noticed among the pretty stones a curious shining reddish material that did not shatter when hit hard with a heavy stone. It merely changed its shape. They soon discovered that they could hammer this interesting stuff, which was raw copper, into useful things. Some of their products, including a gouge and several small sharp pins, were found in the debris of their village. Prior evidence of the use of copper exists in the form of a single bead dating from around 9500 B.C., turned up in a cave in Iraq. But the Cayönü artifacts are the first known tools to be made of any metal.

Almost every neolithic village has yielded to the probing archaeologist other things that are not only unlooked for but defy explanation. Out of the rounded mounds that cover the ruins, deserted thousands of years ago, have come odd-shaped stones of unknown purpose, enigmatic marks and carvings that do not seem to be mere decoration, and human skulls tucked away in odd places. The meaning of these may never be fully known, for they apparently had to do with a vanished religion.

The most ubiquitous of the tantalizing objects to come out of the mounds are small clay figurines, thousands upon thousands of them, that seem to have been part of a "Great Mother" cult. Some are made of unbaked clay or of clay that was burned to brick-like hardness by an accidental fire. Others were deliberately baked in an oven or a kiln, like pottery. The commonest, or at least those that attract most attention, are of naked women, usually enormously fat, with exaggerated breasts, buttocks and thighs (*pages 100-101*). Many appear pregnant. Some archaeologists consider them beautiful and artistically executed. Others see them as crude and ugly. An occasional well-modelled statuette of a woman with a reasonably attractive figure proves in any case that some neolithic sculptors did not lack the necessary skill to create beauty as modern eyes see it.

The most likely explanation for these curious figurines is that they were symbols of fertility. And the neolithic sculptors' emphasis on features connected with childbearing may have been magic intended to keep the village strong and well populated. Women who wanted children may have received such statuettes from priests and put them in a shrine or broken them as a symbolic sacrifice. The idea behind these fertility statuettes was nothing new, even in 10,000 B.C. They bear a strong resemblance to the

Venus figurines of the Cro-Magnons, produced some 10,000 years earlier.

The clay fertility statuettes discovered at Jarmo are fairly realistic; some have faces with eyes, nose and mouth. In others the face is left featureless or the head is reduced to a flat lobe of clay. Sometimes the face is modelled sketchily on a conical clay base without limbs or torso. At Hacilar, in Turkey, an agricultural village that thrived at about the same time as Jarmo, many different varieties of female figurines were found. Often they are simply torsos lacking heads or feet. They are distorted; they writhe. Some are in the position of childbirth.

The fertility cult seems to have persisted right down to classical times. As civilizations developed around the shores of the Mediterranean, a paramount female goddess, the Great Mother, took a prominent place in almost every pantheon. She was Ishtar in Mesopotamia, Ashtoreth in Canaan, Aphrodite in Greece, Venus in Rome. Her mode of worship varied with her worshippers; sometimes she was the goddess of love rather than fertility.

Far back in neolithic times the worship of the Great Mother took an additional form that proved even longer lived. In Hacilar the early stages of this cult are reflected by female figurines that are neither fat nor pregnant, but show a reasonably shaped young woman tenderly holding her child. The figurines may be poorly made and lack beauty, but there is nothing gross about them, and they symbolize not procreation or sex but motherhood. It would be interesting to assemble a series of Madonna-and-Child statues, starting with those created in Hacilar or perhaps even earlier sites and ending with Michelangelo's *Pietà* in the Vatican. Appearances would change, as would

Some Local Variations on the Universal Mother Goddess

Phoenician, ivory, 1500 B.C.   Iranian, clay, c. 1800 B.C.   Phoenician, bronze, c. 1400

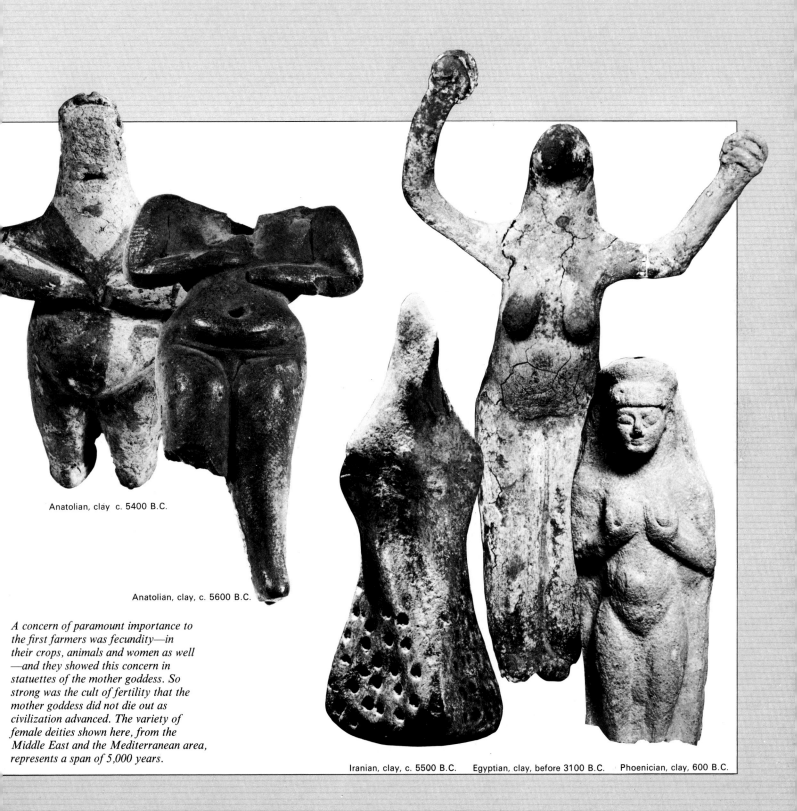

Anatolian, clay c. 5400 B.C.

Anatolian, clay, c. 5600 B.C.

A concern of paramount importance to the first farmers was fecundity—in their crops, animals and women as well —and they showed this concern in statuettes of the mother goddess. So strong was the cult of fertility that the mother goddess did not die out as civilization advanced. The variety of female deities shown here, from the Middle East and the Mediterranean area, represents a span of 5,000 years.

Iranian, clay, c. 5500 B.C.   Egyptian, clay, before 3100 B.C.   Phoenician, clay, 600 B.C.

technique, but the underlying idea of sanctifying motherhood would remain the same throughout.

Not all early Middle East villages produced goddess figurines; some offer almost no evidence of religious practices. But it is unlikely that their inhabitants were nonreligious. Primitive people live in a world dominated by powerful and dangerous spirits that must be appeased or won over. They rarely consider it safe to ignore them. So when a neolithic village seems to have had no religion, this probably means only that the traces of its religious activities have not yet been recognized.

Beidha, the village in Jordan that came to combine farming with rural industries, is interesting on this account. In all of the debris left by some 500 years of occupation, only one Great Mother figurine was found. It seems that the Great Mother did not have many adorers in Beidha. The village did, however, have something that may have been an austere shrine. About 50 yards east of the village proper were found the remains of three remarkable oval buildings that seem to have been built and rebuilt at different stages of Beidha's existence. The middle building is the largest. It is about 20 by 12 feet, paved with small, angular, deliberately broken bits of stone. When the archaeologists unearthed it, the floor was unlittered,

except for a scattering of bone heads. In the centre of the building is a standing stone, a great rectangular block of sandstone from the neighbouring mountains. This centrepiece is three feet high and positioned so its narrower edges face north and south. Two other slabs of stone were set in the floor, or perhaps raised above it on other stones. Another slab was found outside the building, with the remains of a low stone parapet around it. Near by was a roughly triangular limestone slab, 12 feet on its longest side and hollowed out to form a shallow basin.

What was the meaning of these strange structures? Although the Beidhans knew the use of plaster and paint, they seem not to have decorated these stones. It is only a guess, of course, but Beidha's shrinelike place suggests the austerity of the two modern religions that originated not far away: Judaism and Islam. Both forbid the making of "graven images", and Beidha's holy place—if it indeed was that—had none. The symbolic centre of Islam, much older than the birth of Mohammed, is the famous black stone (actually a meteorite) set in the wall of the Kaaba at Mecca. Perhaps the standing stone that the farmers of Beidha erected in the centre of their image-free holy building 9,000 years ago is a distant predecessor of Islam's black stone.

The Flowering of Agriculture in Egypt's Rich Land

Surrounded by farm scenes, a noble couple give thanks for the harvest by anointing an array of fruit, vegetables, bread and meat.

No ancient people raised the art of farming to a higher level than did the Egyptians—nor did any enjoy or appreciate the harvest more. The Egyptians envisioned heaven itself as a place very much like Egypt, where farmers worked the soil and reaped a rich and happy existence. Artists, therefore, were commissioned to paint detailed depictions of farm life to line noblemen's tombs so that the souls of the dead could carry the earth's riches to the afterlife; the symbolic wealth, they believed, would rematerialize in the next world.

Although the tomb paintings were spiritual in purpose, their substance reflects the purely practical aspects of agriculture: how Egypt's farmers prepared their fields for sowing and harvested their crops; how they baked bread and brewed beer out of grains; what livestock they husbanded; the special tools they devised. All are precisely documented by these tomb paintings. The scenes on this and the following pages are based on such art.

Ploughing Fields After the Floods

The annual floods of the river Nile were a kind of giant clock that regulated the lives of Egypt's farmers. In summer, while the waters rose over the land, workers had little farming to do. But in early autumn, when the river had receded enough to expose the silt-enriched fields, ploughing began. There was not a moment to lose, because the soil was easy to plough only while it was still moist. Seed was readied; teams of cattle were yoked; wooden ploughs, some fitted with metal points, were taken out of storage and hauled to the fields. Other workers went along with the ploughmen to help break up clods of mud which were already baking hard in the sun.

Teams of cattle, yoked by a wooden bar over their horns, draw two-handled ploughs through soil enriched with mud deposited by the flooding Nile. The ploughman at left drives his team with a small whip. Other workers (upper panel) fell a tree with an axe and uproot underbrush with a hoe to clear more land for planting. A blue pool of river water, remaining from the inundation, is still standing at the edge of the field.

The Harvest Labours of Men and Beasts

All hands turned out at harvest time and worked from the break of day until nightfall. Men equipped with short-handled sickles reaped the waist-high grain, cutting the stalks about a foot below the ears.

To transport the grain from the fields, the harvesters tied it in sheaves and loaded them in large baskets on-to long-eared donkeys. The animals—amid much balking and braying and considerable beating—then hauled their burdens to threshing floors near by. Competition kept the loading operation brisk: one scribe noted a farmer chiding a co-worker, "I loaded my donkey with 202 sacks while you were sitting on your backside."

A series of vignettes depicts some of the chores of harvesting grain. In the top panel men reap (left) and women winnow some already threshed grain with special scoops (centre); other men fork leftover straw to be stored and used during the coming months for animal fodder, building it into a towering pile (right). The measures for controlling and loading the wilful donkeys are portrayed in the bottom scene.

The Use of Animals Sacred and Scorned

Although cattle were revered in Egypt and associated with gods, and donkeys were disdained as stupid and fractious, both animals had their place as workers on the farm. They were employed in groups on the threshing floors to tread over newly harvested grain, thus loosening the tough chaff from the kernels.

Despite the different attitudes towards them, both ox and donkey were sometimes given bites of grain—and both were subjected at times to harsh words and beatings. When it came time to slaughter animals for food, the respected cattle were more readily sacrificed; their meat—along with their blood—was prized as a delicacy.

Brindled oxen and long-eared donkeys march dutifully over grain on a threshing floor (top panel), an area paved with beaten earth, surrounded by low walls to contain the precious grain. At bottom a crew of butchers, some with whetstones tucked into the waists of their loincloths, dismember four steers with stout, long-bladed knives, while two men stand by with catch basins poised at the ready to collect the blood.

Turning Grain into Bread and Beer

The huge resources of grain in Egypt encouraged bread baking and beer brewing. The Egyptians are believed to have had at least 15 kinds of bread —some of it sweetened with honey. And beer was the country's national drink; it was often carried to the fields in clay jugs as a thirst quencher.

In noble households, most days began with breadmaking. The bakers often used reserved sourdough to produce leavened loaves. The wild yeast in the bread also helped in the beer-making process. Brewers soaked half-baked bread in water, and then added date juice to sweeten the liquid. Foreign visitors compared Egyptian beer favourably with fine wine.

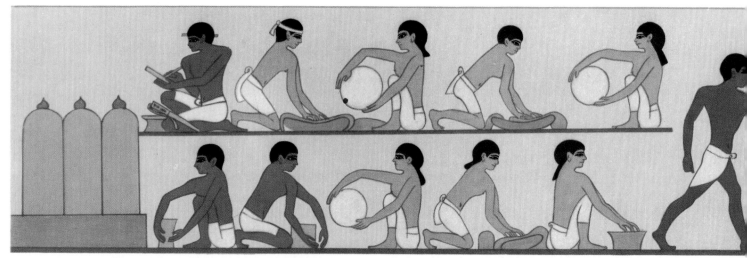

123

Breadmaking is outlined in the upper panel of pictures. First, grain from jars (far left) is ground and sifted while more is pounded in a bowl. After pots are readied for baking and the dough is mixed and kneaded, loaves are baked. Below is shown the brewing of barley beer: at left, date liquor is poured over half-baked bread to hasten fermentation. Then the brewers uncap the jars, pour in the beer, and recap them.

The Ancient Art of Wine Making

Fat, black grapes, the pride of agricultural Egypt, were the source of exquisite wines. Egypt's wine makers were as meticulous about their craft as French vintners are today. The ripe grapes were picked bunch by bunch and carried to the winery in baskets by men—never by pack animals. The first stage of pressing was done in great stone vats; after that, the residue was transferred to sacks of linen and squeezed (*below*) to extract the very last drops of juice. After the wine had fermented, each storage jar was then sealed and labelled with the date, type of wine and names of the vineyard and vintner. One record tells of wine aged for two centuries.

125

The final—and most athletic—phase of grape pressing is demonstrated in this scene. The grapes have already been crushed in vats and the mashed residue has been transferred to a cloth bag which has been twisted tightly. Four men pull on long, crossed poles stuck into the bag's ends, while a fifth, poised spread-legged between the poles, forces them farther apart to squeeze out the last of the juice into a basin.

From the day that man sowed his first crops and domesticated his first animals, it was only a matter of time before his rapidly expanding knowledge enabled him to make great forward strides in agriculture. When nature provided new, adaptable plant hybrids, he could use them to extend farming far beyond the limitations that the earlier varieties had imposed on him. Where rainfall was scarce, he learned to irrigate his fields; and eventually he took to hitching an ingenious invention, the plough, to draught animals and let them pull it for him. He used some of his domesticated animals—the ox, the ass and, ultimately, the horse—to haul goods. Thus, in time he ceased being his own beast of burden and became instead the creator of an emerging civilization, the progenitor of a settled way of life that encouraged the growth of larger and more stable populations.

Not much is known directly about many details of the very earliest cultivation in the Middle East. For example, if there were boundaries delineating the fields around a village like Jarmo, they have long since disappeared, along with any marks of tillage. But it is not hard to reconstruct the problems that the first farmers must have encountered and to guess what the solutions were.

The basic difficulty for these early husbandmen was a matter of the soil itself: as crops were raised in it one season after another, the soil lost its fertility. The effects of the first wheat crops demonstrate

A powerful ox—a descendant of wild cattle domesticated in the Middle East around 6500 B.C.—submits to being harnessed in this impression from a 3000 B.C. Sumerian cylinder seal (the motif is repeated in the impression). The traces are to be hitched to a cart or a plough. Putting cattle to such uses represented one of the great forward strides in agriculture.

the problem. Wheat plants are annuals. Each plant invests in its seeds nearly all the ingested soil nutrients it possesses in order to support the seedlings that will sprout in the next growing season. Then the plant dies. When year after year the seeds and plants are taken away by harvesters (rather than letting the land lie fallow to give it sufficient time to replenish itself with the decomposing plant remains), the soil becomes increasingly impoverished in such critical fertilizing elements as nitrogen, potassium and phosphorus. The crops become less and less vigorous, until they are no longer worth the effort to plant them.

The first farmers could not have understood why their crops diminished. Like primitive farmers of recent times, they simply abandoned the worn-out fields and cleared new land. Yet, knowingly or not, they were practising a crude form of field rotation that, in some areas, had the effect of rejuvenating the land—at least temporarily.

The earliest known farmland, like that around Jarmo in the foothills of Iraq's Zagros Mountains, usually originated in open forest with wild wheat and barley growing among the widely spaced trees. The farmers undoubtedly felled the trees, using stone axes or killing the larger ones by girdling them, cutting rings of bark from their trunks to interrupt the flow of sap. They must have cut the larger bushes and pried small ones out of the soil.

At the end of their rainless summer, when the wood and brush were tinder-dry, they would have cleaned up the fields by lighting fires that burned fiercely, leaving ashes and charred stumps. The soil was thus enriched by such nutrients as potassium and phosphorus from the ashes; and with simple, sharp-pointed digging sticks like those their hunter-gatherer ancestors had used to dig up edible roots and tubers, the farmers stirred up this virgin soil and planted their seeds. The new crop of grain would have grown magnificently, providing a rich harvest. But, inevitably, with the first forest growth gone, the decline in the soil's fertility began again. Meanwhile, the land that had been abandoned earlier would slowly grow up to bushes and trees. The trees would drop leaves and twigs onto the ground, where, through the process of decay, they would deposit nourishing chemicals in the worn-out soil. Other refreshing and essential nutrients would come with the wind and rain. Gradually a layer of humus-rich loam accumulated, and after a period of 20 or 25 years this forest was ready to be cut and burned again to replace the land that had lost its fertility.

This system—called "slash and burn", "forest fallow" or "shifting cultivation"—works pretty well as long as enough land is available. But when the population increases the system may lead to disaster. More and more grain is required to feed the people, so fallow land is brought back into cultivation before it has had time to regain its full fertility. When this happens, the whole system rapidly deteriorates, and soon it can no longer provide enough food to support the farmers and their families.

Many neolithic villages must have suffered such a fate until they were finally abandoned. Yet some farming settlements are known to have persisted in the same area for several centuries. Their inhabitants, then, must have found ways to cope with the dwindling fertility of their fields without abandoning them for a generation or more. What did they do, and how did they discover the answers?

The practices of present-day farming people who still live on a neolithic cultural level indicate what probably happened. One answer to the problem was livestock, which, besides yielding meat and milk, also serve an accessory function. The animals bring plant nutrients from distant pastures and drop them near the village in the form of manure. Human wastes and garbage deposited on the fields can have the same fertilizing effect. In short, the first farmers probably discovered fertilizer without realizing that they had; they may not have understood the benefits of manure, but they profited from it just the same.

The development of improved cultivating tools—spades and hoes with blades of stone, bone or horn—made a difference too. Much more important, however, were improved plant varieties. When wild or semidomesticated wheat is sown by man in prepared soil, it does not have to grow in competition with all the other species, as in the wild. Genetically aberrant seeds that would succumb in the competition of the uncultivated field can now get a chance to grow. And once in a while a few of these aberrations might prove better adapted to the new habitat than the ones regularly planted.

In most cases these improved strains differ little from their ancestors. They just grow slightly better in a colder or drier climate or perhaps in competition with certain other domesticated species. But at long intervals a radically new type might appear, with properties that make it conspicuous and much more valuable to man.

The most important of these more useful plants to appear in the prehistoric world of the Middle East was bread wheat, the type that is still dominant throughout most wheat-growing countries. It originated in a curious way about 8,000 years ago. But the explanation of how this fortunate accident of evolution came about had to wait for the detective work of modern plant geneticists.

Wild emmer wheat is one of the two wild wheat species; the other one is einkorn. Its natural range encompasses Israel, Syria and Jordan. Genetically speaking, it is a tetraploid; that is, it has in its cells 28 chromosomes that carry hereditary characteristics from generation to generation. Bread wheat, however, is a hexaploid, with cells containing 42 chromosomes, and no wheat with this number has ever been found growing wild.

When geneticists investigated where bread wheat's extra 14 chromosomes could have come from, their attention was finally narrowed to *Aegilops squarrosa*, a strain called goat-faced grass because its bristly ear bears a fanciful resemblance to a goat's horns. This variety grows wild in the cool highlands of northern Iran, Afghanistan and far into Central Asia. But because the two species, the grass and the wheat, did not overlap in their natural ranges, they never had a chance to hybridize in the wild.

As the villages and wheat fields of the first farmers spread gradually northwards from the Fertile Crescent, they approached the range of the goat-faced grass. According to plant geneticists, seeds of the goat-faced grass were carried by the wind to the farmers' artificially cleared ground and thrived as weeds among the emmer. Hybridization must thereupon have taken place. Probably most of the early hybrid plants were stunted or otherwise inferior and soon died out. Eventually, though, one unusually vigorous variety appeared. Its seeds were harvested along with those of emmer, and some of them were replanted. Next year there were more of them; and

perhaps after a while they were noticed by observant harvesters who kept them separate for planting in solid stands.

This plant was bread wheat, a hexaploid with 42 chromosomes, 14 of which came from the goat-faced grass. It was superior to emmer in several important ways. For one thing, its seeds lacked emmer's tight-fitting husks, which had to be removed by heating or by pounding in a mortar before the seeds were fit to eat. The farmers' womenfolk surely rejoiced at this lessening of their labour; and the whole family must have appreciated having porridge that was free of scratchy bits of husk. A more important advantage was that bread wheat, unlike emmer, did not require a "Mediterranean" climate with mild, rainy winters and hot, dry summers. From its goat-faced grass ancestor it inherited a tolerance of cold winters and rainy summers. So bread wheat was hardy enough to spread into northern Turkey and Iran, the Balkans and southern Russia, and eventually into northern Europe and Central Asia.

The third advantage of bread wheat, as its name implies, is that it can be made into yeast-raised bread. Emmer and barley too yield bread of sorts. It is still made in the Middle East and is popular with many who praise its flavour. But it is flat, rather like pancakes or Mexican tortillas. What bread wheat has—to a far greater degree than emmer, barley or corn—is a gluten, the gluey material that gives bread its structure and holds in the bubbles of carbon dioxide gas given off by yeast. When ground emmer, barley or corn is mixed with yeast, the dough fails to rise enough to form the light, porous loaves that are the dietary mainstay of Western civilization.

As for yeast, no culinary genius was necessary

to discover it. Wild yeast spores are generally present everywhere as part of the dust in the atmosphere. When dough made of bread-wheat flour is allowed to stand for a day or two in a warm place, it puffs up naturally with bubbles generated by the wild yeast spores carried to it by the air. Perhaps a negligent but stubborn neolithic housewife suspected that her dough might be spoiled when it rose but baked it anyway and was delighted to take from her oven a light, delicious loaf much more attractive and tasty than the unleavened bread she had been accustomed to baking. A second, natural step was for the housewife to save some of the bubbly, unbaked dough, full of living yeast cells, and mix it with the next batch to speed its rising. This is the "sourdough" method of making bread, which was used universally before commercial yeast was available—and is now newly popular among home bread makers.

Bread wheat has been found in archaeological sites dating to 6000 B.C. or so, about a thousand years after the first true agriculture. It may have appeared in as-yet-unexcavated places a good deal earlier, where, it is safe to say, its superior breadmaking qualities were soon noticed and adopted.

But barley was not totally eclipsed by bread wheat, partly because barley too improved over the years. The primitive cultivated barley that was developed by the first farmers was a coarse, prickly grain, with a tightly adherent husk. Although there is no evidence of hybridization to speed the process, cultivated barley gradually became more varied and versatile. From an early and only moderately productive form with two rows of seeds, it developed six rows of seeds. And its close-wrapped husk eventually evolved into one that was much easier to remove.

Under centuries of cultivation, the plant also developed a tolerance to a broad range of climates. Barley is now grown from northern Norway to the edge of the Sahara. In Europe and the United States it is used mostly as an ingredient in making beer, but in parts of the Middle East and Africa, where it is still a principal crop, it is used for bread as well.

Better tools and better crops put Middle East farming on a firm basis, but it was when the villagers learned to irrigate their fields that mankind took a major stride towards true civilization. Irrigation had several extremely important effects. It enormously increased the productivity of agriculture. It enabled farming to spread into arid lands. And since effective irrigation could only be accomplished through the organized co-operation of all the farmers in a village, it also encouraged the development of government and the specialization that goes with it.

Irrigation began as an accidental discovery. Those early Middle East farmers who settled near streams on level, low-lying land soon must have noticed that their crops grew best in spots where the ground was soaked each time the streams flooded. The next step, an easy one, was to improve on nature by leading the life-giving water through furrows from the stream beds to places it did not reach of its own accord.

Luckily for the first irrigators, rivers that flow across level land often build up natural levees. When a river floods and overflows, its heavier silt is deposited near the main channel, while the finer silt is carried farther away. The result after a century or so is a set of high banks confining the river and often raising its bed well above the surrounding plain. It is therefore a relatively simple task to dig a ditch through the natural levee and lead water to flat, eas-

Text continued on page 135

Writing: A Side Benefit from Agriculture

The origin of writing is inextricably tied up with the evolution of agriculture. In the beginning, farmers of the ancient Middle East must have relied on memory to keep track of crops and herds. But as farming became more complex, the problem of recalling what land was whose, who owned which animals and how well the fields and the livestock were producing called for records that could be detailed and durable.

To meet this need, a primitive form of writing was invented around 3000 B.C. in the Middle East. The earliest known examples of written documents are clay tablets from Sumer; their inscriptions, like those at right, are pictorial symbols. Only some of these symbols can be deciphered by modern scholars, but many clearly concern farming: animals, grain and the sun are all represented. These primitive pictograms eventually developed into wedge-shaped characters that became the written code called cuneiform, the first true writing.

Five Sumerian clay tablets, dating back to 3000 B.C., represent the earliest known written records. Their pictograms—a goat's head (1), a stylized cow's head (2), a thresher (bottom of 3) and ears of grain (4 and 5) —imply that they concerned crops and livestock. Large circles (such as at top of 4) evidently mean 100, small circles 10 and long indentations one.

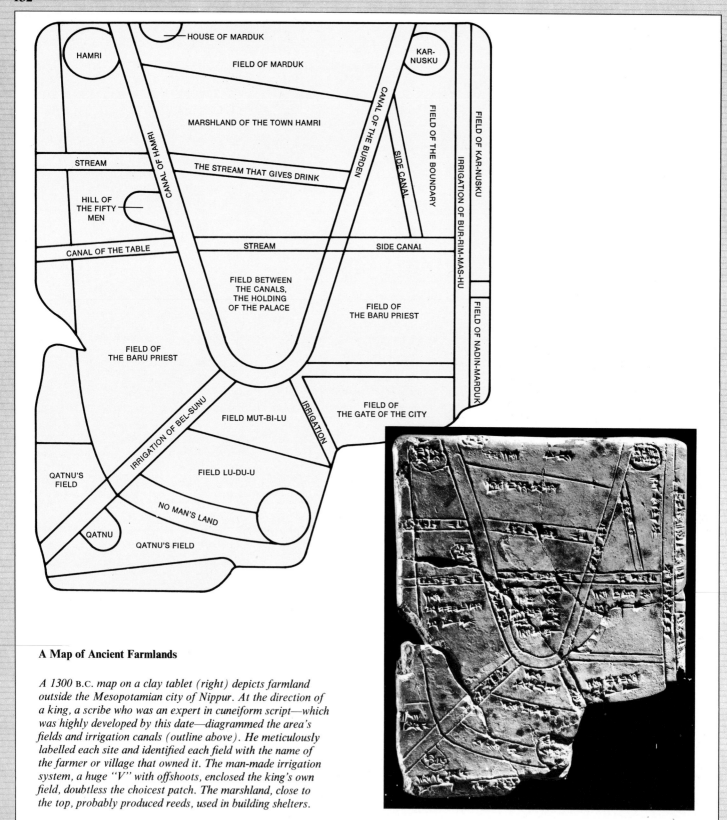

HOUSE OF MARDUK

HAMRI

KAR-NUSKU

FIELD OF MARDUK

MARSHLAND OF THE TOWN HAMRI

FIELD OF THE BOUNDARY

FIELD OF KAR-NUSKU

STREAM

THE STREAM THAT GIVES DRINK

CANAL OF HAMRI

CANAL OF THE BURDEN

SIDE CANAL

IRRIGATION OF BUR-RIM-MAS-HU

HILL OF THE FIFTY MEN

CANAL OF THE TABLE

STREAM

SIDE CANAL

FIELD OF NADIN-MARDUK

FIELD BETWEEN THE CANALS, THE HOLDING OF THE PALACE

FIELD OF THE BARU PRIEST

FIELD OF THE BARU PRIEST

IRRIGATION OF BEL-SUNU

FIELD MUT-BI-LU

IRRIGATION

FIELD OF THE GATE OF THE CITY

QATNU'S FIELD

FIELD LU-DU-U

NO MAN'S LAND

QATNU

QATNU'S FIELD

A Map of Ancient Farmlands

A 1300 B.C. map on a clay tablet (right) depicts farmland outside the Mesopotamian city of Nippur. At the direction of a king, a scribe who was an expert in cuneiform script—which was highly developed by this date—diagrammed the area's fields and irrigation canals (outline above). He meticulously labelled each site and identified each field with the name of the farmer or village that owned it. The man-made irrigation system, a huge "V" with offshoots, enclosed the king's own field, doubtless the choicest patch. The marshland, close to the top, probably produced reeds, used in building shelters.

A Farmer's Profit Statement

A complete accounting of the growth and productivity of a herd of cattle over 10 years in the time of King Sulgi is recorded on this 4,000-year-old tablet, shown front and back. The herd's owner must have managed his farm wisely, for the inscriptions reveal that his herd more than quintupled in size, and the yields of butter and cheese increased accordingly. The second and last year's entries are translated below.

Second year entry:
4 full-grown cows
1 yearling cow
1 suckling female calf
1 yearling bull
1 suckling male calf
butter 20 quarts
cheese 30 quarts
41st year of Sulgi

Tenth year entry:
10 full-grown cows
2 three-year cows
1 two-year cow
2 yearling cows
3 suckling female calves
7 full-grown bulls
1 three-year bull
2 two-year bulls
2 yearling bulls
2 suckling male calves
butter 45 quarts
cheese $67\frac{1}{2}$ quarts
49th year of Sulgi

A Farmer's Almanac for Budding Scribes
Couched in terms of a father advising his son, the text of this tablet outlines the techniques used for raising and harvesting grain. Its instructions could carry a novice farmer through the complete cycle—from preparing an irrigation system to winnowing. It even advises him on how to discipline his labourers. Paradoxically, though, the text was used by student scribes who copied it to perfect their script; learning farming methods was a fringe benefit. A portion of this manual is given below in a free translation.

In the days of yore, the farmer instructed his son: when you are about to prepare the field for irrigation, examine the dikes and ditches to be shored up. On the day when the irrigation waters begin to rise, you would be wise to post a guard over the water-soaked field as herds of oxen must not trample it. When you have weeded the field by hand and worked it over . . . put 10 light copper hoe blades of $\frac{2}{3}$ pound each into good working order; have their handles scored with an axe and lashed with gut.

ily cultivated land below the level of the river. If the stream happens to be a small one, the drain-off of water may cause the stream's level to fall below the level of the irrigated land. In that case, a small dam constructed across the stream below the opening of the irrigation ditch will obstruct the regular flow enough to raise the water level again; it will then resume its flow through the ditch.

Simple irrigation like this is known to have been employed as early as 5500 B.C. in parts of the Fertile Crescent where rainfall was too scant or too erratic for dependable farming. An example can be seen in the region of Khuzistan, a gently sloping plain below the Zagros Mountains of Iran at the head of the Persian Gulf. Throughout the area the courses of long-dried-up streams are lined with the remains of ancient farming villages that are so far from the stream beds that they could not have existed without at least rudimentary irrigation.

As skill in irrigation improved, the villages spread along the streams and out onto the edge of the broad Mesopotamian plain, where the soil was enriched by layers of silt laid down annually by large rivers like the Tigris and Euphrates, but where the natural rainfall was inadequate to support crops. No complicated tools were required to dig channels from the rivers to the fields. A stone-bladed hoe to loosen the earth, a primitive shovel and a stout basket to carry the dirt away were quite sufficient.

But something else was essential: organization. The earliest farmers and their families tilled their own plots. They needed minimal organization to protect their land holdings or pasture rights from aggressive neighbours or enemies.

Irrigated farming was a great deal more complicated. Not only did ditches have to be dug and kept clear of accumulating silt but the water they carried had to be divided equitably among the farmers. Without a strong village authority, there would always be controversy over who was to get what and how to deal with those individuals who tried to take more than their proper share of water.

Thus, partly through dealing with the problem of irrigation, the smaller organizations developed into larger ones. The organized villages that crept slowly out onto the plains of Mesopotamia were the vanguard of the world's first high civilization, that of the Sumerians in the Fourth Millennium B.C. The Sumerian canals were made longer and wider to carry considerable bodies of water. Some of the villages grew into large towns that dominated those around them. Even that fundamental prerequisite to civilization—writing—can be attributed in part to irrigation. In the highly organized towns temples were built for the gods who were believed to control the elements, and writing was invented by the temple administrators among whose duties was keeping records of the food contributed by farmers for the support of the priesthood. Writing was promptly adopted by the farmers themselves to keep their own accounts (*page 133*). Gradually the great city-states evolved—dominated by dynasties of resplendent kings. All of this "hydraulic civilization", as archaeologists sometimes call it, can be credited to the first drought-ridden farmers who led trickles of water from a handy stream.

Neighbouring Egypt was the next region to witness the rise of a hydraulic civilization; and there irrigation developed along different lines. The first neolithic inhabitants of Egypt could not in fact practice farming until they could make use of a form of irrigation because they lacked sufficient rain. They found their compensation in the Nile.

The Nile is a peculiar river; it flows through a narrow, flat-bottomed valley in an otherwise arid desert. Most of the year it carries little water, but early in July its level begins to rise because of heavy seasonal rains in the highlands of Ethiopia, 1,000 miles to the south. By September it floods the valley floor six feet deep or more. Then in October it retreats, leaving the ground covered with a layer of fertile silt. In this moist soil the Egyptian farmers planted their seeds, reasonably sure that there would be enough water left in the ground to nourish their crops. The distribution of flood water, however, was not uniform. Low places got a longer soaking than high ones, and in years when the flood was inadequate the fields near the edge of the flooded areas did not get enough water to sustain plants.

As the valley's population increased, the Egyptian farmers solved the problem of irregular watering by "basin irrigation". First they built low dykes where the river widened into bays, forming basins to trap floodwaters on their return to the river. Then they lined these basins with clay to keep the water from sinking into the soil. Soon they extended these dyked basins to larger areas. By the time of the pharaohs, around 2000 B.C., they had lined both banks of the river and divided the entire Nile Valley into a checkerboard of basins whose water levels could be controlled by sluices. When there was an excess of water in the basins upstream it was drawn off and carried by canals to be used downstream. Other canals led from the basins to the farthest areas to be irrigated. Though heavily used, the well-watered soil never wore out. The silt deposited by the Nile kept it fertile indefinitely.

This elaborate system required a strong, intelligent government to keep the dykes and sluices in repair and to ensure a fair use of the precious water. The irrigated plots were so productive that their crops could support swarms of nonfarmers, and so Egypt provided for artisans, engineers, priests, artists and the architects who built Egypt's temples and pyramids, as well as the courtiers and the pharaohs themselves, who were considered living gods and were treated as such. Egypt's irrigation system made it one of the most successful civilizations in the ancient world. While neighbouring Mesopotamia was subject to damage by salt from saline rivers, which eventually ruined its irrigation system and caused its civilization to decline, the valley of the salt-free Nile has remained productive and densely populated from 5000 B.C. to the present day.

Other parts of the world—Peru, Mexico and China —where agriculture also became the basis for advanced civilizations, owed some of their success to irrigation. In each region it was used in differing ways, but it was a vital element in the people's climb towards a higher level of existence.

On the desert-like coast of Peru rain hardly ever falls, and primitive farming like that of the Middle East was impossible. But in some parts of the Peruvian coast, small, steep rivers plunge down from the Andes to empty their waters into the Pacific. Here, as in the Middle East, the ancient farmers learned to tap the rivers, thereby turning the barren desert soil into richly productive farmland.

The Peruvian rivers resemble the Nile in one way. They rise every year, responding to heavy rain in the

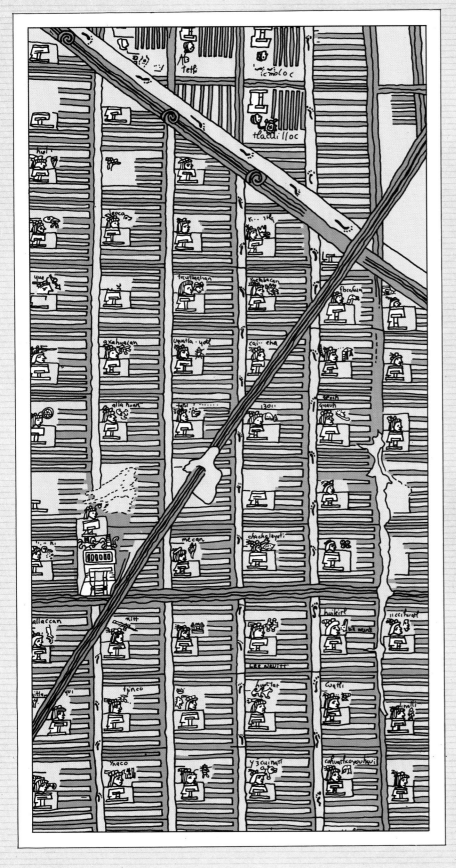

The Island Gardens of Ancient Mexico

A small portion of the gigantic *chinampa* system—the artificial island gardens constructed 2,000 years ago in Mexico—is represented on this map; it is adapted from an Aztec plan of the town that became Mexico City. The blue portions indicate the major canals—many of which could be navigated in flat-bottomed boats—as well as the small channels that mark off each raised plot into a 300-foot-long strip of farmland. The tan areas with footprints are paths. The portrait profiles stand for the homes of the farm owners. Their names appear beside them in Aztec hieroglyphics, some transliterated into Roman letters by a Spanish scribe.

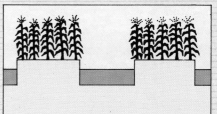

Two of the raised, arable areas (above), from 15 to 30 feet wide, are the "islands" left when the swamp waters are drained off through man-made canals of the chinampa network. Weeds, sediment and mud are piled on top of each island, and the roots of plants—maize, in this case, and trees— help keep the mounds from crumbling.

Andes. In March they are highest, and at this stage they fill their narrow valleys from bank to bank and spread in rivulets over the alluvial deltas built by the silt they have deposited through the ages. The Peruvians planted their crops in these naturally watered areas. They did not build basins to trap water as the Egyptians did, probably because there was not sufficient level land. Instead they used the normal method of irrigation: they dug small ditches that enabled the water to soak into the delta instead of quickly draining off into the sea. As the population increased and food demands grew accordingly, the Peruvians gradually extended their irrigation to higher ground, moving the intakes of the ditches farther upstream and leading the water to areas it had not reached before.

As in the Miidle East, strong local governments helped to build and maintain the Peruvian irrigation systems. In this case the local organizations included the priests of the Peruvians' religion. As early as 2500 B.C., when agriculture was still comparatively crude and much of the food still came from the sea, the coastal villages began to be ruled by priesthoods with power to mobilize the rest of the population for labour. The priests put the people to work on construction projects, especially the impressive religious buildings. Chuquitanta, a village about 15 miles from the Pacific Ocean and not far from the present-day city of Lima, could hardly have housed more than 1,000 people in 2500 B.C., but its relatively few inhabitants, efficiently organized, managed to build a stone-and-mud pyramid-like building whose base measured more than 150 feet square.

Under government control, the Peruvians on the coast carried the irrigation systems back up into their mountain sources. There they diverted the water into lofty ditches that followed the contours of the Andean foothills and irrigated adjacent valleys that had no rivers of their own. Where ravines intersected the ditches, the Peruvians built aqueducts of stone and earth to bridge the gap; one such aqueduct in northern Peru is almost a mile long and 50 feet high. Some of these ancient, mountaineering irrigation systems are as much as 50 to 75 miles long and would be considered enormous engineering projects in any age. Many of them are still in use, and the courses of others can be traced on mountainsides high above the levels of modern cultivation.

The rivers that thus enabled the Peruvians to increase their farming acreage had one serious disadvantage. The water supplied some plant nutrients but lacked the full fertilizing effect of the silt-laden Nile. However, the Peruvians too had discovered the fertilizing properties of manure—in this case guano. The droppings of sea birds, which lived by the millions on rocky islets along the coast, were rich in nutrients. By Inca times the birds' contribution was recognized to the extent that they were protected by law, as they still are today. Their guano, collected and distributed by special government agencies, was applied where it would do the most good, and as a result Peruvian farmland yielded two crops a year.

The ancient Peruvian farmers were ahead of the rest of the world in this respect. The elaborate and highly distinctive civilizations that developed in the little valleys on the rairless coast supported dense populations for 3,000 to 4,000 years, until they were destroyed by the disease and social disruption brought by the Spanish after A.D. 1531.

In Mexico the invention of farming led to even

more spectacular civilizations than in Peru, and in this part of the world irrigation also played an important part in their development. Much more archaeological work must be done to determine when and how it began. But here irrigation took a uniquely Mexican form, particularly in what is now the country's hub, the Valley of Mexico.

During pre-Columbian times this mountain-ringed basin had no natural outlet to carry away the runoff of its rather scant rainfall. The water gradually accumulated in several large lakes. Earlier in the valley's history—perhaps as much as 2,000 years ago —the population on the shore of these lakes evidently grew to the extent that the farmers began to feel pinched for land. So they encroached on the lakes.

Starting in the shallowest places, they drove stakes into the soft bottom and connected them with wickerwork to form small enclosures. Then they scooped up mud and dumped it into the enclosures until they created a scarp of new land rising a foot or so above the water. These always-moist *chinampas* (floating gardens) proved enormously productive and could be planted to crops several times a year (*page 137*). As the population of the Valley of Mexico continued to increase, more and more of them were built. The islands coalesced into blocks of land separated by canals; trees were planted on them so their maze of roots would stabilize the mushy soil, and silt scooped out of the canals was spread on their surfaces to preserve their fertility.

In their peak period, before the Spanish conquest, the *chinampas* were the economic base of the Aztec empire. The gleaming white capital, Tenochtitlán (now Mexico City), was itself built mostly on *chinampas*, and food for its estimated 300,000 inhabitants was brought in from other *chinampa* areas by canoes that plied the canals.

To regulate the water level of the *chinampas* and to protect them from flooding by the salty lakes, the Aztecs constructed a massive dyke of stone and earth that extended for 10 miles. Covered masonry aqueducts leading from springs on the mainland constantly replenished the fresh water without which the *chinampas* could not have functioned properly. The Valley of Mexico is now drained by a canal that releases its excess water to the Pacific Ocean; but some of the *chinampas* are still cultivated in the ancient way. Under the name of the "Floating Gardens of Xochimilco", their canals and abundance of flowers provide a popular resort and a leading tourist attraction for Mexico City.

In China, as in Mexico, the beginnings of irrigation are still unknown. As far as archaeologists have been able to tell, Chinese civilization, already led by a strong government, started without the stimulus of irrigation. And while millet, the first crop cultivated by China's earliest known farmers—in the loess area of the country's semiarid north—would have benefited from irrigation, there is no evidence that the ancient Chinese practised it.

On the other hand, rice, which later became the leading crop of China and Southeast Asia, was almost always grown as it is today, in paddies. To give a high yield, rice needs to have its roots under water. Land that is naturally flooded all year round is rare, however, so the early rice farmers created artificial pools, or paddies, by constructing dykes around low-lying land and diverting water into these enclosures from a near-by stream. Once all the low land was planted to rice, the farmers dug out level paddies on the hillsides, creating the strange stepped landscapes that are a familiar feature of much of China and Southeast Asia.

Irrigation, wherever it was practised by prehistoric farmers, greatly increased the extent and productivity of cultivable land. But there is a limit to the amount of land that can be taken care of with hand tools, especially when a great deal of time must be spent watering it and repairing ditches and dykes. In ancient America the only farm implements were hand tools, and there were no domesticated animals to help the Mexicans and Peruvians with agricultural work; so the farmers' production was indeed limited. For a long time the same held true in the Old World. But all this was changed there by a radical new development: the animal-drawn plough.

The plough itself (*page 141*) was presumably invented in the Middle East, though no one knows exactly when. If it resembled the crude ploughs used by modern primitive peoples, it probably evolved from either digging sticks or hoes. One kind of ancient digging stick that is still used in many areas of the world has a lower end which is bent at an angle like a spade. When a rope is attached a short distance above its point and a man pulls it through the soil, it makes a continuous furrow; another man holds the handle to keep the furrow straight. This man-drawn implement saves little human effort, but speeds up the work. Since there is no English word for it, archaeologists call it an *ard*, which is its Scandinavian name (a very similar one is still used there). Another kind of primitive plough, the *crook-ard*, may trace its ancestry to a hoe made out of a forked limb whose branches joined at an acute angle (*page 143*). When a man drags such a tool through the ground by its longer limb, the shorter limb, armed with a point, digs a furrow.

It was when primitive ploughs like these were hooked up to animals that they became the precursors of the Industrial Revolution—the first tools to be driven by nonhuman sources of power. Instead of depending on human muscles, the farmers now utilized the much stronger muscles of domestic animals. A farmer equipped with a plough and an animal or two to pull it could cultivate much more land in a given time than he had been able to with a hand-driven spade or hoe. The animals, of course, required food to generate their energy, but in those regions where plenty of land was available the animals could forage on acreage that was too poor for farming. So the man-animal combination could produce much more human food than could a man alone, and the surplus could feed the specialized nonfarmers essential for the support of a higher civilization.

But to develop this efficient plough-animal combination, the draught animal had to be trained. Sheep and goats were too small and not powerful enough for the purpose. Horses had the strength, but they were domesticated comparatively late. Thus the plough did not become a very practical farming implement until cattle were turned into animals that could be easily controlled. The date when this was accomplished is unknown, but it was certainly as early as 3000 B.C.

A bull is too unruly to be harnessed to a plough; he must first be converted, by castration, into a placid ox. An animal shown in a Catal Hüyük wall painting in 6500 B.C. lacks a bull's conspicuous testicles and is probably an ox; but it may have been captured in the wild when young, and castrated to make it behave more calmly in religious ceremonials. There is no indication at Catal Hüyük that cattle of any kind

Improvements and Variations on the Plough

Seemingly such a simple tool, the plough was actually one of man's greatest inventions—an efficient, time-saving device that was improved with minor changes as farming evolved. The first ploughs were essentially crude hoes dragged by hand through the soil. Then came a variety of useful adaptations and attachments, ranging from handles to seed-planting funnels—plus the addition of draught animals. Although the ploughs, made of wood, rotted away long ago, archaeologists know how they looked. The illustrations at right are based on the ancient pictorial word symbols for the ploughs themselves; the original symbols accompany the illustrations.

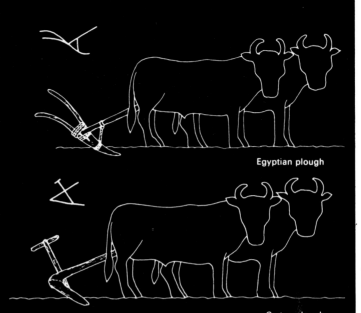

Egyptian plough

Cretan plough

A two-handled plough and its related pictogram (top) show how Egypt's ploughs looked around 3000 B.C. In Crete, around 2000 B.C., farmers used a steering handle (above) to leave one of the ploughman's hands free to prod the oxen. Mesopotamian farmers, driving oxen joined to a yoke shaped like the four-barred pictogram below, added a funnel, seen in the drawing. Seeds were poured through the funnel into furrows made by the plough. The centre panel of the Assyrian bas-relief at left, from 670 B.C., shows this efficient invention.

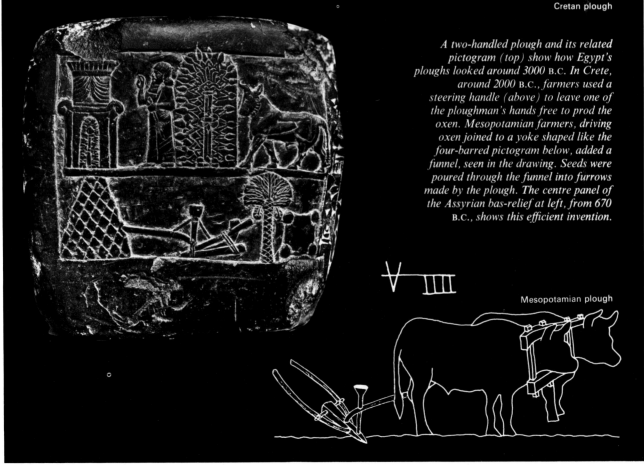

Mesopotamian plough

were used as draught animals. So the earliest proof so far uncovered that ploughs were being drawn by oxen is in depictions of them found in Mesopotamia and Egypt, dating about 3000 B.C. The oxen shown hitched to the ploughs are small and presumably the products of a long process of selection for small size and docility. Thus the ox-drawn plough may be a deal older than this first bit of evidence.

No physical traces of ancient ploughs survive; and these early pictures of them show why: they were constructed of perishable wood. In 3000 B.C. iron was still too rare to be put to such use. The renderings also show that the ancient ploughs were little more than larger and heavier versions of the primitive man-powered *ard* or *crook-ard* to which a handle for steering had been attached, with a forward-pointing pole tied directly to the animals' horns or to a beam lashed across them. At a later date the double-neck yoke, which seems to have been used first for ox-drawn wagons, was applied to ploughs as well, making it possible for the farmer to utilize the great power in the neck and shoulders of the ox.

Eventually, simple animal-powered ploughs spread from the Middle East and Egypt through Asia and North Africa and as far north in Europe as Scandinavia, where they are depicted in rock drawings dating back to about 400 B.C. Basically unchanged, they are still used not only in underdeveloped countries but also for special cultivating tasks in advanced countries. Sometimes they merely make furrows in the ground, or they may be tilted so that they throw most of the soil to one side. Simple ploughs like these were the predecessors of the true plough, equipped with a wheel in front to keep its point from plunging too deeply into the soil, and with a moulded board above the ploughshare to turn over a strip of soil, let the air in and bury most of the weeds at the same time.

With the development of the plough, the man-plant-animal symbiosis that helps to sustain nearly all humankind was essentially complete. Plants contributed food. Animals contributed food, fertilizer and traction. Man contributed an ever-decreasing amount of muscle power and an ever-increasing amount of knowledge, skill and management. All three partners benefited and multiplied enormously at the expense of wild species. And thus, thousands of years before the appearance of industrialism, man and his symbionts had conquered the earth.

Living Replicas of the First Farmers

An Ethiopian farmer heads towards his field. His plough, made from a sapling, is like those used by Middle Easterners 5,000 years ago.

While in some parts of today's world farmers have become used to such sophisticated machinery as harvesting combines and crop-dusting aeroplanes, many millions of souls work their land as their prehistoric ancestors did. Ethiopians use carved wooden ploughs that are similar in design to those depicted in Fourth Millennium B.C. Egyptian art. South Pacific islanders still employ the slash-and-burn technique to make virgin land ready for their crops. In India and Southeast Asia, where many archaeologists believe that early farmers originated the technique of transplanting rice seedlings to flooded fields called paddies, the rice-cultivation method used 5,000 years ago persists unchanged today. In the Middle East winnowing grain is often done by hand, and in Central and South America it is not unusual to see people grind grain with a type of stone board and rolling pin that was first invented some 5,000 years ago.

The fact that so many of the ancient techniques and tools are still used testifies to their efficient simplicity. They —and these patient, productive contemporary people—provide a window into the past, a clear view of the ways in which the first farmers worked their ancient lands.

Watering the Land

*To get the most out of the land in an almost arid region,
farmers in Bihar, India, dip water from a stream into irrigation
ditches lining their wheat and potato fields. The device they
use, called a denkli, is a simple well sweep, with a bucket
hung from a counterweighted bar balanced on a forked post.
A similar device appears in 1500 B.C. pictures from Egypt,
where it may have been invented—and it is also still in use.*

Winnowing Grain

*Employing a method that originated in the prehistoric Middle
East, village women in Afghanistan winnow wheat to remove
chaff from kernels. The grain, which has been threshed, is
first thrown into the air with forks; as most of the light chaff
blows away, the heavier kernels fall back. Next the grain
is shaken in these tambourine-shaped sieves to sift out
remaining chaff, then the kernels are heaped on the ground.*

Herding Flocks

Mottled goats are prodded home by a young goatherd after a day of grazing in India's dusty Punjab region. Over the centuries, goats have been among the most economical animals to raise. They eat almost anything that grows; their hair is good for weaving, their milk and meat are nutritious. In fact, goats have been almost too much of a good thing in parts of Asia, where their incessant grazing has destroyed ground cover and encouraged erosion of once-arable land.

Transplanting Rice

Gracefully bent like dancers, six sari-clad women work a paddy in Bihar, India. Rice, the crop by which the Indians live or die, is still cultivated in many parts of Asia by methods first used at least 5,000 years ago in China. The seeds are sown in dry fields, and when the sprouts are about a foot tall, they are transplanted one by one to artificially flooded paddies. Harvesting the full-grown grain is also done by hand.

148

Threshing Grain

A farmer in Egypt's Nile Delta drives his bullock-drawn thresher over a heap of wheat sheaves to free the kernels from their tough casings; the boys ride along to add extra weight. The thresher —invented in the Mediterranean area 3,000 years ago—has circular blades mounted on a roller between runners. The machine represents a double revolution in early farming: the mechanization of threshing, which had formerly been done by humans or animals trampling the grain, and the use of draught animals to drag heavy gear.

Grinding Grain

In Guatemala two Indian farm women use one of the oldest known milling methods to grind corn for tortillas—the flat bread that is the staple of their diet. Their stone grinding implements, called piedras de molar in Spanish and saddle stones in English, are nearly identical to one depicted in an Egyptian carving that dates back to 2700 B.C. The same implements also survive in Africa and the Middle East.

Baking Bread

Using a method as old as baking itself, a peasant woman in Iran prepares nan-e sangak—a flat bread made of wheat, flour and water. After she shapes the dough into discs, she bakes them in a clay oven sunk halfway into the ground (page 44); the oven is jointly owned and used by all the families in her village. She also strategically arranges five heated pebbles on top of the dough to help cook it through.

Scaring Off Scavengers

Perched on top of a precarious tower of sticks rising out of a crop of durra—a grain similar to millet—an Ethiopian woman serves as a human scarecrow. To prevent monkeys from running wild over the crop and eating the young grain, she hurls stones at them. Early farmers the world over probably dealt with animal marauders in a similar fashion—except that, unlike modern Ethiopians, they probably aimed to kill and supplemented their food supply by eating their target.

Clearing a Field

On a hillside sloping into the Pacific Ocean, aborigines on Pentecost Island finish preparing a patch of virgin land for a yam crop after using the ancient slash-and-burn method. The field was first cleared of its larger trees by hacking them down with axes, killing them by stripping a belt of bark from their trunks or prying them up by the roots. The remaining brush and saplings were then burned off; the burning also enhances the mineral richness of the island's volcanic soil.

The Emergence of Man

This chart records the progression of life on earth from its first appearance in the warm waters of the new-formed planet through the evolution of man himself; it traces his physical, social, technological and intellectual development to the Christian era. To place these advances in commonly used chronological sequences, the column at the

Geology	Archaeology	Thousand Millions of Years Ago	
Precambrian earliest era		4.5	Creation of the Earth
		4	Formation of the primordial sea
		3	First life, single-celled algae and bacteria, appears in water
		2	
		1	
		Millions of Years Ago	
			First oxygen-breathing animals appear
		800	
			Primitive organisms develop interdependent specialized cells
		600	Shell-bearing multicelled invertebrate animals appear
Palaeozoic ancient life			Evolution of armoured fish, first animals to possess backbones
		400	Small amphibians venture on to land
			Reptiles and insects arise
			Thecodont, ancestor of dinosaurs, arises
Mesozoic middle life		200	Age of dinosaurs begins
			Birds appear
			Mammals live in shadow of dinosaurs
			Age of dinosaurs ends
		80	
			Prosimians, earliest primates, develop in trees
Cainozoic recent life		60	
		40	Monkeys and apes evolve
		20	
		10	Ramapithecus, oldest known primate with apparently man-like traits, evolves in India and Africa
		8	
		6	Australopithecus, closest primate ancestor to man, appears in Africa
		4	

Geology	Archaeology	Millions of Years Ago	
Lower Pleistocene oldest period of most recent epoch	**Lower Palaeolithic** oldest period of Old Stone Age	2	Oldest known tool fashioned by man in Africa
		1	First true man, Homo erectus, emerges in East Indies and Africa
			Homo erectus populates temperate zone
		Thousands of Years Ago	
Middle Pleistocene middle period of most recent epoch		800	Man learns to control and use fire
		600	
		400	Large-scale, organized elephant hunts staged in Europe
			Man begins to make artificial shelters from branches
		200	
Upper Pleistocene latest period of most recent epoch	**Middle Palaeolithic** middle period of Old Stone Age		Neanderthal man emerges in Europe
		80	
		60	Ritual burials in Europe and Middle East suggest belief in afterlife
			Woolly mammoths hunted by Neanderthal in northern Europe
		40	Cave bear becomes focus of cult in Europe
	Upper Palaeolithic latest period of Old Stone Age		Cro-Magnon man arises in Europe
			Asian hunters cross Bering Land Bridge to populate New World
			Oldest known written record, lunar notations on bone, made in Europe
			Man reaches Australia
			First artists decorate walls and ceilings of caves in France and Spain
		30	Figurines sculpted for nature worship
		20	Invention of needle makes sewing possible
			Bison hunting begins on Great Plains of North America
Holocene present epoch	**Mesolithic** Middle Stone Age	10	Bow and arrow invented in Europe
			Pottery first made in Japan

Last Ice Age

▼ Four thousand million years ago   ▼ Three thousand million years ago

▲ Origin of the Earth (4,500 million)   ▲ First life (3,500 million)

left of each of the chart's four sections identifies the great geo-ical eras into which the earth's history is divided by scientists, le the second column lists the archaeological ages of human his-y. The key dates in the rise of life and of man's outstanding omplishments appear in the third column (years and events men-tioned in this volume of The Emergence of Man appear in bold type). The chart is not to scale; the reason is made clear by the bar below, which represents in linear scale the 4,500 million years spanned by the chart—on the scaled bar, the portion relating to the total period of known human existence (*far right*) is too small to be distinguished.

Geology	Archaeology	Years B.C.	
olocene (ont.)	**Neolithic** New Stone Age	9000	
			Sheep domesticated in Middle East
			Dog domesticated in North America
		8000	Jericho, oldest known city, settled
			Goat domesticated in Persia
			Man cultivates his first crops, wheat and barley, in Middle East
		7000	**Pattern of village life grows in Middle East**
			Catal Hüyük, in what is now Turkey, becomes largest Neolithic city
			Loom invented in Middle East
			Cattle domesticated in Middle East
	Copper Age	6000	**Agriculture begins to replace hunting in Europe**
			Copper used in trade in Mediterranean area
			Corn cultivated in Mexico
		4800	Oldest known massive stone monument built in Brittany
		4000	Sail-propelled boats used in Egypt
			First city-states develop in Sumer
			Cylinder seals begin to be used as marks of identification in Middle East
		3500	**First potatoes grown in South America**
			Wheel originates in Sumer
			Man begins to cultivate rice in Far East
			Silk moth domesticated in China
			Egyptian merchant trading ships start to ply the Mediterranean
			First writing, pictographic, composed in Middle East
	Bronze Age	3000	Bronze first used to make tools in Middle East
			City life spreads to Nile Valley
			Plough is developed in Middle East
			Accurate calendar based on stellar observation devised in Egypt
		2800	Stonehenge, most famous of ancient stone monuments, begun in England
			Pyramids built in Egypt
			Minoan navigators begin to venture into seas beyond the Mediterranean
		2600	Variety of gods and heroes glorified in *Gilgamesh* and other epics in Middle East

Geology	Archaeology	Years B.C.	
Holocene (cont.)	**Bronze Age** (cont.)	2500	Cities rise in the Indus Valley
			Earliest written code of laws drawn up in Sumer
			Herdsmen of Central Asia learn to tame and ride horses
		2000	Use of bronze in Europe
			Chicken and elephant domesticated in Indus Valley
			Eskimo culture begins in Bering Strait area
		1500	Invention of ocean-going outrigger canoes enables man to reach islands of South Pacific
			Ceremonial bronze sculptures created in China
			Imperial government, ruling distant provinces, established by Hittites
		1400	Iron in use in Middle East
			First complete alphabet devised in script of the Ugarit people in Syria
			Hebrews introduce concept of monotheism
	Iron Age	1000	**Reindeer domesticated in Eurasia**
		900	Phoenicians develop modern alphabet
		800	Celtic culture begins to spread use of iron throughout Europe
			Nomads create a far-flung society based on the horse in Russian steppes
			First highway system built in Assyria
			Homer composes *Iliad* and *Odyssey*
		700	Rome founded
			Wheelbarrow invented in China
		200	Epics about India's gods and heroes, the *Mahabharata* and *Ramayana*, written
			Water wheel invented in Middle East
		0	Christian era begins

Two thousand million years ago

One thousand million years ago

First oxygen-breathing animals (900 million)

First animals to possess backbones (470 million)

First men (1.3 million)

Credits

The sources for the illustrations in this book are shown below. Credits from left to right are separated by semicolons, from top to bottom by dashes.

Cover—Painting by Burt Silverman, background photograph by David Rubinger. 8 —Dr. Georg Gerster from Rapho-Guillumette. 11—Map by Rafael D. Palacios. 12, 13 —David Lees, TIME-LIFE Picture Agency, © 1964 Time Incorporated. 16, 17, 18—Anthony Howarth from Woodfin Camp & Associates. 23—Tor Eigeland from Black Star. 25 to 33—Paintings by Jack Endewelt. 34—Aldo Durazzi courtesy Archaeological Museum, Nicosia. 38—Courtesy Dr. W. Van Zeist, Rijksuniversiteit, Groningen, The Netherlands. 40, 41—Drawings by George V. Kelvin. 42, 43—Aldo Durazzi courtesy The Iraqi Museum, Baghdad except far top right, Ara Guler courtesy Ankara Archaeological Museum. 47 to 51—Richard Jeffery. 52—Henry B. Beville courtesy Library of Congress, Hispanic Collection. 55, 56, 57 —Courtesy The Institute of Archaeology, Academia Sinica, Peking, China. 59—Dr. Umesh C. Banerjee, Harvard University except far left column, Elso S. Barghoorn, Harvard University. 63 to 66—Paulus Leeser courtesy Rare Book Division, The New York Public Library, Astor, Lenox and Tilden Foundations. 68—Robert Colton courtesy University Museum, University of Pennsylvania. 70, 71—Paulus Leeser courtesy American History Division, The New York Public Library, Astor, Lenox and Tilden Foundations. 74—Ara Guler courtesy Ankara Archaeological Museum. 76, 77—Maps by Lothar Roth, animal drawings by Earl L. Kvam. 79—Courtesy of the Trustees of the British Museum. 81—Robert Colton courtesy Smithsonian Institution. 82, 83—Brian Hesse courtesy Faunal Research Group, Department of Anthropology, Columbia University except far bottom left, Robert Colton courtesy Faunal Research Group, Department of Anthropology, Columbia University. 84—Robert Colton courtesy Smithsonian Institution —Robert Colton courtesy Field Museum of Natural History, Chicago. 87—Pierre Boulat courtesy Musée du Louvre, Paris. 88, 89 —Aldo Durazzi courtesy The Iraqi Museum, Baghdad. 90—Juan Guzman, TIME-LIFE Picture Agency, © 1956 Time Incorporated— No credit. 91—Hirmer Fotoarchiv, Munich —Ashmolean Museum, Oxford. 94—Ara Guler courtesy Ankara Archaeological Museum. 100, 101—Aldo Durazzi courtesy The Iraqi Museum, Baghdad. 104, 105—Painting by Nicholas Fasciano. 107 to 110— From *Excavations at Hacilar* by James Mellaart © 1970. British Institute of Archaeology, Ankara. Edinburgh University Press except left page 107, Ara Guler courtesy Ankara Archaeological Museum. 112—Lauros-Giraudon; Giraudon; Archives Photographiques. 113—Ara Guler courtesy Ankara Archaeological Museum; Courtesy University Museum, University of Pennsylvania; Jiri Jiru courtesy Royal Museum of Art and History, Brussels; Lauros-Giraudon. 115 to 125—Renderings by James Alexander based on photographs courtesy Giraudon. 126 —Curtesy of the Trustees of the British Museum. 131—Staatliche Museen zu Berlin Vorderasiatische ABT (East Berlin). 132 to 134—Paulus Leeser courtesy University Museum, University of Pennsylvania. 137—Adapted from *The Chinampas of Mexico* by Michael D. Coe. Copyright © 1964 by Scientific American, Inc. All rights reserved. 141—Courtesy of the Trustees of the British Museum; From *Technology in Archaeology* by Henry Hodges, illustrated by Judith Newcomer. © 1970 by Henry Hodges. Reprinted by permission of Alfred A. Knopf, Inc. 143 —Dr. Georg Gerster from The John Hillelson Agency Ltd., London. 144—Raghubir Singh from Woodfin Camp & Associates. 145—Roland and Sabrina Michaud from Rapho-Guillumette. 146, 147—William MacQuitty —Cary S. Wolinsky from Stock, Boston. 148, 149—Tor Eigeland from Black Star. 150 —Douglas Faulkner. 151—David Lees. 152 —Kal Muller from Woodfin Camp & Associates. 153—Dr. Georg Gerster from Rapho-Guillumette.

Acknowledgments

For the help given in the preparation of this book the editors are particularly indebted to Jack R. Harlan, Professor of Plant Genetics, Department of Agronomy, University of Illinois, Urbana; Charles A. Reed, Professor, Department of Anthropology, University of Illinois at Chicago Circle, Chicago. The editors also express their gratitude to Afral Armed, Curator, Archaeological Museum, Mohenjo-Daro, Pakistan; Umesh Banerjee, Research Fellow, Arnold Arboretum, Elso S. Barghoorn, Fisher Professor of Natural History, Department of Biology, Harvard University, Cambridge, Massachusetts; Erna Bennet and Charles Voss, United Nations Food and Agriculture Organization, Rome; Ignacio Bernal, Director, National Museum of Anthropology and History, Mexico City; Kwang-chih Chang and Michael D. Coe, Professors, Department of Anthropology, Yale University, New Haven, Connecticut; Maud D. Cole, Rare Book Room, The New York Public Library, New York City; Frederick Collier, Collections Manager, Department of Paleobiology, Smithsonian Institution, Washington, D.C.; Department of Western Asiatic Antiquities, British Museum, London; Christopher B. Donnan and Henry B. Nicholson, Professors, Department of Anthropology, University of California at Los Angeles; Georgette Dorn, Research Librarian, Hispanic Section, Library of Congress, Washington, D.C.; Gordon F. Ekholm, Curator of Mexican Archaeology, American Museum of Natural History, New York City; Richard Fazzini, Assistant Curator of Egyptian and Classical Art, Brooklyn Museum, New York City; Kent V. Flannery, Professor, Department of Anthropology, and Curator, Museum of Anthropology, University of Michigan, Ann Arbor; Ignace J. Gelb, Frank P. Hixon Distinguished Service Professor of Assyriology, Oriental Institute, University of Chicago; Diane Harlé, Myriam Odier, Françoise Tallon and Geneviève Teissier, Louvre Museum, Paris; Brian Hesse; Charles F. W. Higham, Professor, Department of Anthropology, University of Otago, Dunedin, New Zealand; Ping-ti Ho, Professor, Department of History, University of Chicago; Barbara Lawrence, Curator of Mammals, Museum of Comparative Zoology, Harvard University; Richard S. MacNeish, Director, Robert S. Peabody Foundation for Archaeology, Andover, Massachusetts; Albina De Meio, Keeper, American Sections, and Ake Sjoberg, Clark Research Professor of Assyriology, University Museum, University of Pennsylvania, Philadelphia; James Mellaart, Lecturer in Anatolian Archaeology, Institute of Archaeology, London; Gerhard Rudolf Meyer, Director-General, Berlin State Museum, Berlin; Kyriacos Nicolaou, Curator, Nicosia Archaeological Museum, Nicosia, Cyprus; Zechiya Ongur, Turkish Embassy, Rome; Dexter Perkins Jr., Research Fellow, Patricia Daly, Faunal Research Group, Department of Anthropology, and Isabella M. Drew of Sackler Laboratory, Columbia University; Jane Renfrew, Visiting Lecturer in Archaeology, University of Southampton, England; Dr. M. L. Ryder; Niaz Rasool, Director, National Museum of Pakistan, Karachi; Issa Salman, Director, and Fawzi Rashid, Iraq Museum, Baghdad; John Paul Scott, Centre for Research on Social Behaviour, Bowling Green State University, Bowling Green, Ohio; William Solheim, Professor, Department of Anthropology, University of Hawaii; Raci Temizer, Director, Archaeological Museum, Ankara, Turkey; Giuseppe Tucci, President, and Raffaeli Biscione, Lorenzo Costantini, Marcello Piperno, Maurizio Tosi, Italian Institute of Middle and Far East, Rome; Priscilla F. Turnbull, Field Museum of Natural History, Chicago; Maurits N. van Loon, Professor in Archaeology and Prehistory of Western Asia, Institute of Prehistory and Protohistory, Amsterdam; Willem van Zeist, Professor, Institute of Biology and Archaeology, State University, Groningen, The Netherlands; Gordon Willey, Professor of Anthropology, Peabody Museum, Harvard University.

Bibliography

General Studies

Boserup, Esther, *The Conditions of Agricultural Growth: The Economics of Agrarian Change Under Population Pressure.* Aldine Publishing Co., 1965.

Braidwood, Robert J. and Gordon R. Willey, eds., *Courses Toward Urban Life.* Edinburgh University Press.

Brothwell, Don and Erick Higgs, eds., *Science in Archaeology.* Thames and Hudson, 1970.

Clark, Grahame, *World Prehistory: A New Outline.* Cambridge University Press, 1969.

Clark, Grahame and Stuart Piggott, *Prehistoric Sciences.* Hutchinson, 1965.

Coon, Carleton S., *The Hunting Peoples.* Little, Brown and Co., 1971.

Curwen, E. Cecil, *Plough and Pasture.* Cobbett Press, 1946.

Duran, Diego, *Book of the Gods and Rites and the Ancient Calendar.* University of Oklahoma Press, 1971.

Forbes, R. J., *Studies in Ancient Technology,* Vol. VI. E. J. Brill, 1958.

Fussell, G. E., *Farming Techniques from Prehistoric to Modern Times.* Pergamon Press, 1966.

Gelb, Ignace J., *A Study of Writing.* University of Chicago Press, 1952.

Hodges, Henry, *Technology in the Ancient World.* Allen Lane, 1970, Penguin, 1971.

Lee, Richard B., and Irven DeVore, *Man the Hunter.* Aldine Publishing Co., 1968.

Matson, Frederick R., ed., *Ceramics and Man.* Aldine Publishing Co., 1965.

Singer, Charles, E. J. Holmyard, A. R. Williams and I. Trevor, eds., *A History of Technology.* Oxford University Press, 1967.

Spooner, Brian, ed., *Population Growth: Anthropological Implications.* M.I.T. Press, 1972.

Steward, Julian H. et al., *Irrigation Civilizations: A Comparative Study.* Pan American Union, 1955.

Tringham, Ruth, *Hunters, Fishers and Farmers of Eastern Europe, 6000-3000* B.C. Hutchinson University Library, 1971.

Ucko, Peter John, Ruth Tringham and G. W. Dimbleby, eds., *Man, Settlement and Urbanism.* Duckworth, 1971.

Washburn, Sherwood L., *Social Life of Early Man.* Aldine Publishing Co., 1961.

Wulff, Hans E., *Traditional Crafts of Persia.* M.I.T. Press, 1971.

Domestication

Broderick, A. Houghton, ed., *Animals in Archaeology.* Barrie and Jenkins, 1972.

Fiennes, Richard and Alice, *The Natural History of Dogs.* The Natural History Press, 1970.

Higgs, E. S., ed., *Papers in Economic Prehistory:*

Studies by Members and Associates of the British Academy Major Research Project in the Early History of Agriculture. Cambridge University Press, 1972.

Hill, Albert F., *Economic Botany: A Textbook of Useful Plants and Plant Products.* McGraw Hill, 1952.

Isaac, Erich, *Geography of Domestication.* Prentice-Hall, 1971.

Peterson, R. F., *Wheat.* L. Hill, 1968.

Renfrew, Jane M., *Palaeoethnobotany: The Prehistoric Food Plants of the Near East and Europe.* Methuen and Co., 1973.

Sauer, Carl Orton, *Agricultural Origins and Dispersals.* M.I.T. Press, 1969.

Schwanitz, Franz, *Origin of Cultivated Plants.* Harvard University Press, 1966.

Struever, Stuart, ed., *Prehistoric Agriculture.* Natural History Press, 1971.

Ucko, Peter J., and G. W. Dimbleby, eds., *The Domestication and Exploitation of Plants and Animals.* Duckworth, 1969.

Vavilov, N. I., *The Origin, Variation, Immunity and Breeding of Cultivated Plants.* Translated from the Russian by K. Starr Chester. The Chronica Botanica Co., 1949-1950.

Wickizer, Vernon Dale, and M. K. Bennett, *The Rice Economy of Monsoon Asia.* Food Research Institute, Stanford University, 1941.

Zeuner, Frederick E., *A History of Domesticated Animals.* Harper & Row, 1963.

Regions: Old World

Braidwood, Robert J., *Prehistoric Man.* Scott, Foresman and Company, 1967.

Braidwood, Robert J., and Bruce Howe, *Prehistoric Investigations in Iraqi Kurdistan.* University of Chicago Press, 1960.

Chang, Kwang-chih, *The Archaeology of Ancient China.* Yale University Press, 1968.

Childe, V. Gordon, *New Light on the Most Ancient East.* Routledge and Kegan Paul, 1958.

Higham, C., and M. Jurisich, *Prehistoric Investigations in Northeast Thailand, 1969-1970.* University of Otago, New Zealand, 1970.

Ho, Ping-ti, *Loess and the Origin of Chinese Agriculture.* Hong Kong University Press, 1969.

Hole, Frank, Kent V. Flannery and James A. Neely, *Prehistory and Human Ecology of the Deh Luran Plain.* University of Michigan, Museum of Anthropology, Memoirs, No. 1. Ann Arbor, 1969.

The Institute of Archaeology, Academia Sinica, ed., *The Neolithic Village at Panp'o, Sian.* The Wen Wu Press, 1963.

Lucas, A., *Ancient Egyptian Materials and Industries.* Edward Arnold, 1962.

Mallowan, M. E. I., *Early Mesopotamia and Iran.* Thames and Hudson, 1965.

Mellaart, James, *Earliest Civilizations of the Near East.* Thames and Hudson, 1965. *Excavations at Hacilar.* Edinburgh University Press, 1970.

Montet, Pierre, *Everyday Life in Egypt.* St. Martin's Press Inc., 1958.

Perkins, Dwight H., *Agricultural Development in China.* Edinburgh University Press, 1970.

Porter, Bertha and Rosalind L. B. Moss, *Topographical Bibliography of Ancient Egyptian Hieroglyphic Texts, Reliefs and Paintings.* Oxford University Press, 1964.

Posener, Georges, *Dictionary of Egyptian Civilization.* Tudor Publishing Co., 1959.

Pritchard, James B., *The Ancient Near East in Pictures.* Princeton University Press, 1970.

Treistman, Judith M., *The Prehistory of China.* The Natural History Press, 1972.

Watson, William, *Early Civilization in China.* Thames and Hudson, 1966.

Regions: New World

Baumann, Hans, *Gold and Gods of Peru.* Translated by Stella Humphries. Oxford University Press, 1963.

Bennett, Wendell C., and Junius Bird, *Andean Culture History.* Natural History Press, 1964.

Bushnell, G. H. S., *Peru.* Thames and Hudson, 1963.

Byers, Douglas S., ed., *The Prehistory of the Tehuacan Valley.* University of Texas Press, 1968.

Caso, Alfonso, *The Aztecs: People of the Sun.* University of Oklahoma Press, 1967.

Coe, Michael D., *Mexico.* Thames and Hudson, 1962.

Lanning, Edward P., *Peru before the Incas.* Prentice-Hall, 1968.

MacNeish, R. S., A. Nelken-Terner, and A. G. Cook, *Second Annual Report of the Ayacucho Archaeological-Botanical Project.* Robert S. Peabody Foundation, 1970.

Mason, John Alden, *The Ancient Civilizations of Peru.* Penguin, 1969.

Means, Philip A., *Ancient Civilizations of the Andes.* Gordian Press Inc., 1964.

Sahagún, Bernardino de, *Florentine Codex, General History of the Things of New Spain.* Translated and edited by Charles E. Dibble and Arthur J. O. Anderson. The School of American Research and the University of Utah, 1950-1970.

Stirling, Matthew W., ed., *Indians of the Americas.* National Geographic Society, 1955.

Vaillant, George C., *Aztecs of Mexico.* Penguin, 1965.

Wauchope, Robert, ed., *Handbook of Middle American Indians.* University of Texas Press, 1970.

Willey, Gordon R., *Introduction to American Archaeology, South America.* Prentice-Hall, 1972.

Index

Filmsetting by C. E. Dawkins (Typesetters) Ltd., London, SE1 1UN
Printed and bound in Belgium by Brepols Fabrieken N.V.